THE JESUS OPTION

Reflections on the Gospel for the C-Cycle

Joseph G. Donders

ORBIS BOOKS
Maryknoll, New York 10545

The Catholic Foreign Mission Society of America (Maryknoll) recruits and trains people for overseas missionary service. Through Orbis Books Maryknoll aims to foster the international dialogue that is essential to mission. The books published, however, reflect the opinions of their authors and are not meant to represent the official position of the society.

Library of Congress Cataloging in Publication Data

Donders, Joseph G.
  The Jesus Option.

  1. Bible. N.T. Gospels—Meditations. I. Title.
BS2555.4.D66   242'.3   82-2241
ISBN 0-88344-243-4 (pbk.)   AACR2

To

Saint Paul's Catholic Community
University of Nairobi

and

Saint Michael's Catholic Community
Kabete University Campus

CONTENTS

INTRODUCTION

The story of Jesus
has been told
for almost
two thousand years.
It will be told
for all the years
to come.
 It has been told
 in all kinds of ways.
 So many approaches
 are possible:
 the older ones
 crystallized in
 creeds and catechisms;
 the newer ones
 shown in liberation
 and materialistic interpretations.
But whatever we do
with his story,
whether we dogmatize,
intellectualize, emotionalize,
psychologize, or rationalize it,
it should remain
the story
about him.
 He should remain
 in the center,

1

and to take him
in the center
is what we have tried
to do
at Saint Paul's Catholic Community
at the University of Nairobi
in Kenya,
while telling his story
again
according to the Gospel readings
of liturgical cycle C,
mainly taken
from the Gospel of Luke.
We did not try
to make him
the center of our sympathy only
because *we* and *our* sympathy
would have remained in the center
of our interest.
We did not try
to see him
as our friend,
though he certainly is,
because *we* and *our* friendship
would have remained
the focal point.
We did not try
to see him
as our brother,
though his blood flows through us,
because *we* and *our* brotherhood
would have been the point
of our interest.
We did not try
to see him
as our Master,
though we owe our allegiance to him,
because *we* and *our* servanthood
would have remained

the main issue
under study.
We tried to see him
as he was and is and will be
in himself.
We tried to walk
in his shoes;
we tried to get
into his feelings;
we tried to penetrate
his thoughts;
we tried to put ourselves
in his place
to make him,
in that attempt of
empathy,
real to us.

That attempt
might seem to be
presumptuous or preposterous.
It is
in a way.
But did Paul not write
that Jesus was equal
to us
in all
but sin?

Doing this
we were struck,
especially while reading Luke,
by his concern
for this world;
by his care
for the poor;
by his option
in favor of those,
whether poor or rich,
who live
their divinely given lives

in frustration and
agony.
We were struck
by his option.
We were struck
by his alternative.
We were struck
by him:
our human fellow-being,
our friend,
our brother,
our Master.
And we hope
to be able
to draw
the conclusions
of this being struck by him
in the practice
of our lives,
sharing his option
and his alternative.

1.

THE END AT THE BEGINNING

Luke 21:25–28, 34–36

Today we start again
to tell the story
of Jesus of Nazareth,
that wonderful human being,
that Son of God
called by all of us
Christ,
the anointed one,
the chosen one.
>This story has been told
>again and again
>year after year
>for almost two thousand years.
>That is one of the reasons
>that he remained with us,
>that he lives with us;
>but it is not
>the only reason.
It might sound strange
that we begin this story

5

with his announcement
of the end
of this world.
> He speaks
> about a sun
> that is fading away.
> He speaks about stars
> losing their shine.
> He speaks about an end
> that according to him
> unavoidably will come.
> He speaks about men and women
> at a total and final
> loss.
Why do we start
by telling about
that end?
> But, brother or sister,
> or all you who hear:
> is not every story
> about an end
> also a story
> about
> a beginning?
Is the last day not always
the dawn of
a new day
to come?
> Is a last look
> at the past,
> at the house
> you leave,
> at the dead
> you bury,
> not always
> followed
> by a look
> into the future

at the things
to come?
When he, Jesus,
speaks about that end,
he is thinking of a world
that is going to disappear,
that world of corruption and sin,
that world of hatred,
jealousy, greed, apartheid, war, and murder
we all know
so very well,
as it surrounds us
as our second
skin.
When he, Jesus,
speaks about the end
of this world,
he is foretelling
the new world
to come,
a better one,
a different one,
the kingdom of God
in which we
too
will be changed.
Some call this
only a dream,
and they are wrong
because they have
no hope.
Others hold
that he only meant
the new heaven to come,
and they too neutralize
what he really said
and meant
by adding things like:

"That end
will come
in four years' time,
in five years maybe,
but surely
in the year
2000!"
It is then,
those prophets say,
that God
in an all-ending wrath
· will finish this world,
burning it
away.
But is that
what he meant
when he spoke
and said:
"The new kingdom is
among you"?
Is that what he meant
when he said:
"Go out into this world
and preach,
baptizing it
in the name of the Father
and the Son
and the Holy Spirit"?
Is that what he meant
when he broke his bread
and shared his wine
in that hall there and then,
telling them
to share like that
all through this world
remembering him?
He did not only speak
of a new heaven
to come.

He also spoke
about a new world
to be formed.
A world recreated
in his Spirit,
and by his Spirit
given
to us.
Come, let us break up,
the dark is
almost over,
the dawn
is very near.

2.

A VOICE IN THE WILDERNESS

Luke 3:1–6

John
was the name
of the voice
that was sent to shout
in a world
that had been described
by so many prophets
before that John
as a wilderness,
a jungle.
> He was the voice of the Lord,
> a voice
> heard no longer
> in a world
> where the original goodness
> of the sky and the earth,
> of the water and the air,
> of the fire and the light,
> of the oils and the minerals,
> of the flowers and the trees,
> of the animals and their young,

10

of its men and women
had been practically
lost.
At the moment that the things
came out of the hands
of God,
at the moment that he and she
came out of those hands
the Lord said:
"How good is all this
as conceived,
ordered,
and made
by us."
But they,
he and she,
responded
by saying:
"Let us
determine
by ourselves,
what is good and
what is bad.
We don't need a god
for that."
And eating from that tree
of knowledge
reserved to God alone,
the whole tree of life
grew awry
in jungle-like fashion
with offshoots and
undergrowths,
with wild growths and
overgrowths
in dissolution,
in sickness and death.
And they themselves,
he and she,

decided
that they were
naked,
and so they
were.
>   But now that voice
>   was heard
>   speaking about an axe
>   lying at the roots
>   of that sick tree,
>   speaking about
>   restoration
>   and the filling of holes,
>   speaking about straightening
>   and leveling,
>   about sifting and sorting out,
>   about pruning and weeding,
>   about liberation and salvation,
>   about a new life
>   and a new spirit.

And the sky and the earth,
and the water and the air,
and the fire and the light,
and the oils and the minerals,
and the flowers and the trees,
and the animals and their young,
and all men and women,
the whole of creation,
were bathed in hope and joy.
>   A radiant light
>   was and is
>   on its way
>   in that darkness
>   of ours.

3.

WHAT SHOULD WE DO?

Luke 3:10 –18

John the Baptist
announced
a total change.
The old tree of life
was going to fall,
the old disorder
would disappear.
> People were enthusiastic,
> they thronged around him,
> a feeling of expectancy
> had grown
> all over the land.
But,
what did they expect?
How did they think
that the new order
would come?
> I think that we can check
> the answers they gave
> with our own life experience.
> Let us take the church
> we belong to:

13

twice in 1979
we had a new start.
Twice expectancy
grew.
Twice everybody was
enthusiastic:
the new order
will start.
New life will be
given.
Pope Paul VI
had grown very old
and very sick.
He said
—with a very painful face—
at every reception he gave:
"I am very happy
to see you,"
but his face
showed no happiness
at all.

> After Paul's death
> we got John Paul I,
> smiles all over,
> hope, faith, and charity galore,
> but he died
> so soon.

Then came
John Paul II.
He too smiled
and he traveled
more around this world
in one year
than all the other popes
maybe did
together.

> In a few months' time
> he gave
> dozens and dozens
> of speeches,

often in very troubled spots
like Ireland.
It seemed
that there would be
peace
in that divided country.
There are reports
that bombs were
laid down,
that the prostitutes
lost their patrons,
and that churches
filled up.
Expectancy grew.
But then,
very soon,
all returned
to "normal"
again
and even a church
the pope had blessed
was bombed,
it seems.
      But,
      what did he expect?
      How did he think
      that the new order
      would come?
The Gospel of John
gives the answer.
The people came
to John
to ask:
"What should
WE
do?"
      There were the tax collectors,
      those profiteers of the old order,
      who came to ask him:
      "What should WE do?"

Soldiers,
the stubborn defenders
of the old relationships,
came to ask him:
"And what about US?"
They came to ask him
not
what should our officers
do;
they came to ask him
not
what should the minister of finance
do;
they came to ask him
not
what should others
do;
they came to ask him:
"What should we
ourselves
do?"

And John answered.
He said:
"Anyone who has two tunics
while others have none
should share,
anyone who has something to eat
should do
the same."
John did not ask
for what we might call
scientific socialism
or a self-propelling liberalism.
John asked
for much
more.

Brothers and sisters,
we are full of expectations,
that is true.

But are we willing
to expect that change
of ourselves?
Are we willing to grow
in that direction
ourselves?
Very many of you
are willing to share
within the circle of your families.
The shirts you are wearing now
are often faded and old
because your brother or sister
needed a school-uniform,
a pair of shoes,
or some socks.
But are we willing
to make that sharing
our policy
all over this world?
No wonder
that John
added
that SPIRIT and FIRE
would be given to us
personally,
internally,
to help us
to realize
our dreams.
Spirit and fire
to us
in ourselves
to be able to change
this world.
Because
without that change in us
we would not be able to change
this world
at all.

At least
not according to John,
and he knew
what he was talking about,
because,
as Jesus said,
John was the greatest
of all
in that old order
of humankind.

4.

ABOUT THE SEED
THAT GROWS

Luke 1:39–44

In those days
Mary,
full of Holy Spirit
and her son to be born,
went to her cousin, Elisabeth,
she too
full of Holy Spirit
and her son to be born.
> Mary
> was in a very special
> situation:
> in her
> all newness
> was developing,
> out of her
> all newness
> was going to be
> born.
But around her
all went on
in the old-fashioned way,

in Nazareth,
in Palestine,
in the world.
        It was as if
        everything was happening;
        it was as if
        nothing was happening
        at all.
        Nobody paid any attention
        to her.
        She was alone
        with her filled womb
        and the promise,
        even while she was walking
        all the way
        to that cousin Elisabeth.
When the Roman security-forces
stopped her
she thought:
"If only
you knew."
When she went to buy
some food,
she thought:
"If only
you guessed."
        But nobody
        knew
        and nobody
        guessed.
She knew.
She believed.
Joseph knew.
Joseph believed.
But next to them,
who else did?
And what did even
Joseph
really
know?

Nothing, nothing happened
up to the moment
that she met
Elisabeth
and the contents
of Elisabeth's old womb,
John.
It was that John
who kicked her
with such force
that she cried out:
    "Blessed,
    blessed,
    blessed,
    you who believed
    that the promise made
    will be fulfilled!"
We,
who are preparing
to celebrate
Christmas
in this world
in which we live,
    do we believe,
    like Mary,
    that Jesus
    was planted
    into this world,
    in us?
Do we believe
in the power
of that seed
planted
in this world?
Do we believe
in its promise?
    All seems to be
    as usual.
    No change seems
    to have been made.

All seems to be
as always,
neither better
nor worse.
The coming year will make
no difference.
And if there would be
a difference,
then things only promise
to be worse:
a world
on the point of
collapse:
no oil,
electrical blackouts,
no food,
but weapons
all over.
Some weeks ago
I was asked to give a talk.
I said that I thought
that goodness in our world
is growing,
but I got some
quite angry remarks
telling me
that things are worse
than ever
before.
If that is true,
what about God's Spirit
in this world?
If that is true,
what about God's power
invested in us?
What about the seed
in the womb of Mary?
What about the seed
in the womb of this world?

If we don't believe
in the seed,
how will it then
be able to grow
in us
and in this world?
You can find out
for yourself
what will happen
when we don't believe,
when we don't encourage
each other.
Take two pots
with earth.
Put in each one
some beans
and let them grow.
Put the pots
in separate rooms
and go
every day
a few times to those seeds
to speak to them.
Say to one set:
"You are doing fine,
I believe in your power,
look how you are growing,
I believe in your strength!"
Tell the other set:
"You are hopeless,
no growth at all,
I don't believe in your power,
I don't believe in your strength,
be cursed and die!"
And see what happens:
the first set will grow
straight up and nice;
the second set will wither,
mixed up and confused.

Brothers and sisters,
let us believe in the power
and the strength
of what we are celebrating
these days,
let us encourage
each other
and goodness will grow,
and life will be victorious
and he will be born,
Alleluia!

5.

ANGELS MADE THE DIFFERENCE

Luke 2:1-14

Mary
had walked
quite a way
and Joseph
too.
They finally
arrived
at Bethlehem,
and,
thanks be to God,
they found a place
to stay.
>Even before
>they had had the time
>to arrange and organize
>anything properly,
>her labor began
>and Jesus was born
>into this world.

Mary knew
what really happened
to this world
at the moment
he was born
because an *angel*
had appeared to her.
Joseph knew
what really happened
to this world
at the moment
he was born
because an *angel*
had appeared
to him
even more
than once.
But nobody else,
except Elisabeth and John,
knew anything
at all.

      People had, of course,
      noticed
      that Mary was pregnant,
      so what?
      People had, of course,
      noticed
      that Joseph accompanied her
      everywhere,
      but wasn't that
      to be expected?
      People knew
      that a baby was due,
      but wasn't she
      in her ninth month?
Nobody noticed
anything special
at all.

They were all turning
in the small circles
of their own lives,
of their own thoughts.
That small circle of birth,
       growth,
       children,
       and death.
A bit like hens
around which one
has drawn
circles in the sand
and who
looking at those circles
do not move
anymore.
              It was in those small circles
              too
              that the shepherds
              were sitting
              around their fires,
              with their sleeping sheep,
              in another circle,
              around them.
              They were leading
              rather uneventful lives,
              without too much hope,
              without an escape,
              very frustratedly
              herding sheep of others,
              destined to play
              no role
              in human history
              at all,
                   until
                   those *angels*
                   appeared
                   to them.

At that moment
their human dimensions
were opened up.
At that moment
they were suddenly
in the light
and saw.
At that moment
the circles around them
broke up,
and a new beginning
was born in them,
full of
hope.
      The circles
      in which we
      ourselves
      are turning,
      herding the things
      in this world,
      are very often very narrow
      indeed.
      Those circles
      are not only narrow,
      but also so little
      hope-giving:
          hunger and thirst,
          inflation and unemployment,
          frustration and hollowness,
          prostitution and underdevelopment
      and nobody knows
      how to get out of them.
      We all seem to be caught and
      trapped,
      encircled and
      hemmed in,
      like those shepherds
      in the dark and the cold
      around their dying fires.

But tonight
those *angels*
appear to US.
Their appearance
is an invitation
to break through
our circles.
The first thing
they say
is:
"Don't be afraid."
And the second thing
they tell us
is:
"We bring you
news
of great joy,
a new child,
a savior,
has been born
to YOU!"
        When you look
        at that first Christmas crib
        in Bethlehem
        all seems perfectly
        normal:
            there is a mother,
            there is a father,
            there is a baby,
            there are some visitors,
            there is a donkey,
            there is an ox,
            there are some chickens
            and a dog,
            the normal
            circle and
            cycle,
                but then
                there are those *angels,*

                    and they
                    really
                    indicate and make
                    the difference.
Those *angels*
will disappear,
they will fly away
again,
but
they leave us
with their message.
They announced
what they had to announce.
What they announced
was supposed
to be sufficient
to make those shepherds
move
out of the cocoon
of the daily lives
in which they had been
living.
                    That is what
                    they did,
                    they broke up
                    to go to that child.
                    We should do the same,
                    finding new meaning
                    in our lives.

6.

PEACE AND ITS PROBLEMS

Luke 2:1–14

When he was born
the first word of the angels
was
PEACE.
His own first word
after his death and resurrection
was
PEACE.
His first interest
and his last interest,
his only interest
seems to have been that
PEACE.
      The people around him
      did not show the same interest.
      There is no incident
      in any of the four Gospels
      where anyone is asking him
      for peace.
They say:
      "I am blind,
      let me see."

They say:
>"I am deaf,
>let me hear."

They say:
>"I am lame,
>let me walk."

They make signs:
>I am mute,
>let me speak.

Others say:
>"My daughter,
>my son,
>my brother is dead,
>let her,
>let him live."

But no one speaks
even with one word
about
PEACE.

>And we,
>do we really pray
>for PEACE,
>except when wars and riots
>threaten our eyes,
>>our ears,
>>our limbs,
>>our throats
>>and our lives?
>Aren't our health,
>>our good fortune,
>>our examinations,
>>our careers,
>>our toothaches and
>>headaches,
>the only subject of
>our prayers?

And nevertheless
Pope John Paul II
said in his 1979
New Year's message:

"On this day
that opens
the new year,
it is not possible
to utter a wish
more fundamental
than the wish for
PEACE."
That is true.
But to be able to understand
that fully,
we must remind ourselves of
what the opposite of
PEACE,
of what its negation,
WAR,
really means.
War is the total collapse
of all humanity,
of all morality,
of all decency,
of all mutual respect:
we suddenly think
that we are allowed to
KILL.
Even the most pious
and religious person,
all at once,
does not seem
to be bound
by any command or vow
anymore:
we behave worse
than animals,
we do not only kill,
we overkill.
We should pray for PEACE,
but that PEACE
is not something
hanging in the air;

it is not something idle
or abstract.
In our official Roman Missal
practically any prayer for PEACE
is combined
with a prayer for
JUSTICE.

      If we want PEACE
      then we should be willing
      to help to organize
      this world
      in such a way
      that no one feels tempted
      to secure one's human rights
      with violence.
You might say:
"Why pray for peace
in Kenya?
Is that,
our country,
not peaceful and
stable?"

      It is true:
      no bombs
      are exploding
      over here.
      It is true:
      nobody dies of
      shrapnel wounds.
But it is
at the same time
not true.
Because
bombs have to be bought
over here in Kenya
because of the type of world
we live in.
Those bombs
have to be paid for,

and money can only be spent
once.
And because of the money
to be paid
for those bombs,
no efficient or no more help
can be given
in this country
to the starving,
the socially frustrated,
and the uneducated.
And in that way,
those bombs,
though they do not explode,
do kill
and maim.
People do die
because of
them.

      It is true
      that this country Kenya
      is not at war
      internationally.
      But it is not only
      on those battlefields
      that wars are fought.
Think about the families
in disarray
fighting among
themselves.
      Think about the violence
      in the streets,
      the lack of security,
      the gap between the rich and the poor,
      the competition in the schools,
      the inequalities,
      the envy and the hatred.
Let us all pray for
PEACE,

let us all work for
JUSTICE and
PEACE.
>PEACE
>was the first word
>about
>him,
>PEACE
>was his
>last word.

Let us pray,
forgiving the past,
changing in the present and
organizing a more
PEACE-FULL
future.
Amen.

7.

HE WANTED TO BE BAPTIZED

Luke 3:15–16, 21–22

The first thing
Jesus did
when leaving Nazareth
was to walk
in the direction of
John the Baptist.
    When he arrived
    hundreds of others
    were queuing up
    in front of that
    prophet.
He joined
at the end
of the queue.
It was a strange queue.
It consisted of people
who were convinced
that they were sinners.
It consisted of people
who were convinced
that the world in which
they lived
was no good,

37

or not so very good
at all.
> They were hoping
> that something drastic
> would happen
> in their lives
> and in this world.

John had been baptizing
for weeks
on end.
He had been giving
advice,
he had been
counseling.
He had washed
sin after sin,
and yet,
now and then,
a doubt crept
into his own
mind.
> What he did,
> did not mean too
> much.
> What he did
> related only
> to the past
> and a bit to the present
> but it did not promise
> anything
> for the future
> really.

He was washing wounds,
but the sickness remained.
He was scratching
the surface
only.
> And so he,
> himself rather upset,
> started to tell them:

"It is not I
who am going to change
this world.
It is not I
who am going to solve
your problems.
There must be
someone else.
It is not
this water
that can do it.
It is his fire
and his Spirit."
And he was waiting
from moment to moment,
and from person to person,
for that other
one.
Until Jesus
knelt
in front
of him.
Until heaven opened
and a voice was heard
and the Holy Spirit
descended on
him.
Before that voice
was heard,
he had knelt
in the mud
in front of
John.
It is important
to understand
that it was
while kneeling
in that mud
that he heard
that voice.

Because this means
that the mud
was intended
and that the mud
was touched
when the heavenly voice
spoke.
That mud signified
the drabness
of the world
in which we live,
its evil and
its sin.
Here,
in this chapel,
very clean,
beautiful,
with nice flower arrangements,
pleasant people,
a shimmer of gold
and real (imported) marble,
we run the risk
that we overlook
the mud
in which he knelt,
overlooking too
what he really came to do
in our world.
Instead of between flowers,
he was kneeling in the mud
of the dresses of the poor,
their smell, their sweat,
and their fleas.
Instead of between flowers,
he was kneeling in the mud
of the headlines of our papers,
fornication and rape,
adultery and murder,
theft and shootings.

Instead of between flowers,
he was kneeling in the mud
of the smoke of guns,
missile sites and military bases,
hand grenades and the neutron bomb.
Instead of between flowers,
he was kneeling in the mud
of the tears of children
who failed impossible examinations.
Instead of between flowers,
he was kneeling in the mud
of our whispered confessions
of hatred and envy,
of exploitation and betrayal.
It was
in that mud
that he stepped.
It was
out of all that mud
that he stepped
when that voice
was heard,
and God said:
"You are my beloved
son,
in you
I am very pleased."
The Lord intervened,
the Spirit came down
and John jumped up
to make a place
for the newness
that started,
ready to be
the prisoner
of a past
that gave way
that day
and hour.

8.

FIRST TO THE WEDDING
AT CANA

John 2:1–12

The story for today
is very simple.
Jesus visited some people
who were celebrating
their wedding.
A very common occurrence,
so common in fact
that even the names
of the two
are not mentioned.
> The wine got finished.
> Some say
> because Jesus came in
> with those sailors
> following him.
> He compensated
> the bride and the bridegroom
> with seventy-five crates
> of wine.

What does this report mean?
Why did he do this?
It is very difficult
to try to answer those questions
from books written
by learned specialists
on this matter.
>They speak about it
>in very mysterious
>and mystical terms.
>They seem to turn
>the whole episode
>into an enigma,
>a riddle,
>a problem,
>in which the two
>who are married
>are totally
>lost.
No author talks
about them,
though Jesus came
obviously
for them.
>They only ask questions like:
>"Why did he call his mother
>'woman'?"
>"What did that saying
>'my hour' mean?"
>And they start to reason then
>about the mystical marriage
>between God and his people,
>they start to speculate
>on the change in the role of Mary
>from mother to bride
>in all kinds of esoteric
>and high-flying
>interpretations.

I do not say
that you cannot read
the Cana story
at that level.
You can read texts
at all kinds of levels.
But I do think
that for that very reason
you can read it also
at another level,
a more normal one.
Our level,
my level,
your level.

      Last Sunday
      we saw Jesus
      queuing up before John.
      John,
      who told everyone
      who was ready to listen,
      that this whole world
      should change.

Jesus agreed
with that point of view.
That is why he too
queued up
in front of John
waiting his turn.
That is why he too
knelt
in the mud and the sin
of this world.

      Heaven opened
      in approval and affirmation,
      a voice was heard and
      a mission given.

He got the message
and disappeared in the desert.

He was tempted
to run away
from it all.
He overcame the temptations
that lasted for forty days.
He came out of the desert,
into the jungle of this world.
He picked some followers
and started his ministry
by going,
according to John,
first to the wedding
at Cana.
          Why?
          Was it to indicate
          in an unmistakable way
          where the renewal,
                    the revolution,
                    the healing and
                    the restoration
          should begin?
When Mother Teresa
got the Nobel Prize
for Peace
some time ago
the journalists
who surrounded her
asked:
"What is according to you
the way to a lasting
peace?"
She answered them
very shortly
in four words only:
"A good family life."
          She was right,
          though the reporters seemed to be
          disappointed.

She was right.
The quality of human life
depends essentially
on how marriages
work out.
Human life itself
depends on it.
What were the two in Cana,
what are the persons
who marry in Nairobi,
hoping for,
she and he,
he and she?
They hope
that they may get
life
in at least two ways:
life from each other
life for each other,
life for their children,
life from their children.
Life from each other,
life for each other,
she helping him,
he comforting her,
he boosting her,
she stimulating him.
Life for their children,
life from their children,
not only at the moment of birth,
but in that slow process
in which a family grows
up.
Jesus did not want to be
misunderstood
on that point,
though he remained
unmarried himself.

And that might have been
the real reason
that the first thing he did,
when starting his redeeming work,
was to go
to that couple
in Cana.
It is very good to pray
for all kinds of things,
for success in examinations,
for a brilliant career,
for a fruitful service,
but don't forget to pray
for a good husband
or for a good wife,
don't forget to pray
for your husband
or for your wife:
    your life
    and that of your offspring
    will depend
    on him
    or
    on her!

9.

ARE WE GOOD NEWS
TO THE POOR?

Luke 4:1-4, 14-21

He had been baptized.
The Holy Spirit,
the Spirit of God,
had descended on him.
He fled into the desert,
tempted to give up or
not even to start.
He did not give in.
He came out of the desert.
He picked some company
and went then
to that wedding at Cana
to indicate
where the foundation
of human life lies.
>When passing through Cana
>he must,
>according to Luke,
>have been on his way
>to his hometown,
>Nazareth.

His fame had been spreading
already
and on that first Sabbathday
in Nazareth
everyone who could move
in that town
went to the synagogue.
They were curious
and they definitely expected
him there,
because,
as Luke wrote:
"It had been his custom
to be there,
on the Sabbathday."
  When the leader
  asked for a reader,
  they all remained
  very determinedly
  seated.
  No one
  stood up.
  They wanted him
  to stand up and
  to take the reading.
And that is
what he
did.
  He stood up.
  He took the book.
  It was no book
  but a scroll.
  They handed him the scroll
  of the prophet Isaiah.
  He accepted their choice.
  He took the scroll.
  He rolled it down
    —a hush went all through
    the building—
  and he read:

"THE SPIRIT OF THE LORD
HAS BEEN GIVEN TO ME,
FOR HE HAS ANOINTED ME.
HE HAS SENT ME TO BRING
THE GOOD NEWS TO THE POOR,
TO PROCLAIM LIBERTY TO CAPTIVES
AND TO THE BLIND NEW SIGHT,
TO SET THE DOWNTRODDEN FREE,
TO PROCLAIM THE LORD'S YEAR OF FAVOR."

He then rolled up the scroll,
gave it back to the assistant,
and sat down
        —another hush went all through
        the building:
        only teachers with authority
        sat down
        while speaking.
He said:
        "This text is being
        fulfilled today,
        even as you listen."
        "The time
        has come!"
When we hear this text
we Christians might get up
very enthusiastically,
and this enthusiasm and excitement
is very often
and very rightly
present in a student community.
And off we go
through the campus,
through the streets,
in the direction of parliament
and the office of the *Daily Nation*
or the *Standard*
shouting
        that others
        should do justice
        to others;

shouting
  that others should be
  of the Spirit of God,
  just and fair,
  charitable and loving.
And that is true.
They really should.
But let us not forget
that it is WE too
who are baptized in him
and washed and converted
and filled with that Spirit of God,
the Spirit of Jesus Christ.
  It is clear
  from the text
  read by Jesus in Nazareth
  what that Spirit should do
  in us.
  It should do in us
  what it did in Jesus:
    Bring good news
    to the poor,
    liberate captives,
    give sight to the blind,
    uplift the exploited
    and proclaim God's grace.
It means
that wherever we find
any human being
not fully living up
to his or her human dignity,
that wherever we find
a fellow human being
dehumanized,
we should help
that brother or sister
to be fulfilled,
whatever the reason
of dehumanization
might have been:

psychological,
spiritual,
physical,
medical,
economic,
or cultural.
We should be like him,
as far as we can,
helping,
enlightening,
and uplifting.
And according to Jesus himself
we shall even be judged
according to what we
did.
In the end he will say:
"There was a human being
who was hungry.
You could easily have helped.
What did you do?
There were those others in prison,
not only in prison physically,
but in prison
     psychologically and
     spiritually and
     so on.
What did you
do?"
     In the end he will say:
     "You met me,
     Jesus,
     dehumanized,
     disabled,
     exploited,
     wounded,
     hungry,
     handicapped,
     unemployed,
     a school dropout,

a refugee,
and what did you,
what did your community
do?"
Are we really
good news
to the poor,
to him?

10.

HIS UNFORGIVABLE INCLUSIVENESS

Luke 4:21–30

While he spoke in that synagogue
in Nazareth,
his townspeople
were astonished
by his words,
and they said:
"How right he is,"
and they added:
"What a blessing to us
over here in Nazareth,
isn't he the son of Joseph,
a man of this town?
What a blessing to us,
how greatly our community
will profit."
> That is what they said,
> but in their hearts,
> in the local bars,
> in the kitchens,

and in the workshops
they had been blaming him
already.
They had been gossiping
about him
all over the place.
He could work miracles,
so far so good,
but why had he given them
that wine in Cana
of all places?
What about their own
thirst in Nazareth?
Why those healings
in Capernaum?
What about the sick
in the street where he had lived
for so long?
Why all those
spectacular things
among strangers
and foreigners,
why had he not come home
immediately
after that baptism
they all had heard about?
Was he not Joseph's son,
did he not belong to them,
was he not of their flesh
and of their blood?
> He should be ashamed of himself.
> He should change his attitude.
> He should change himself.
> He should heal himself.
> He should stay with them.
He knew them very well.
He knew their thoughts exactly
and he said:

"No doubt
you want to tell me:
heal yourself,
do the things you did
up to this moment
elsewhere,
now
over here.
Stay with us,
restrict yourself
to your own
circle."
"No doubt
you want to tell me:
when you gave them
all that wine in Cana,
we over here were
very thirsty.
How could you think
of them
and forget about us?
Haven't we been drinking
with you,
while you were here
with us?
Shame on you!
Shame!"
"No doubt
you want to tell me:
while you were healing
in Capernaum
there were sick people
over here
in your own town,
in your own family.
What do you think
they thought when they heard
that you were healing
elsewhere,

   losing your time
   in far-off places?
   Shame on you!
   Shame!''
They wanted to restrict him
to themselves
only.
They wanted to bind him
to his blood-group
only.
They wanted him to take
that attitude
that causes almost
all the trouble
in this world:
   apartheid,
   nationalism,
   fascism,
   racism,
   tribalism,
   nepotism,
   and elitism.
He told them:
''That time is over.
That sin should have been
overcome
by now.
Even the prophets of old
showed already
that all this is of
the past.
What about Elijah?
   There were very many widows
   in his day,
   starving with their children
   in the land of Israel.
   But he did not help them,
   he helped a foreign one
   in Zarephath.

What about Elisha?
> There were very many lepers
> in his day,
> suffering bitterly
> in the land of Israel.
> But he did not help them,
> he helped an alien one,
> Naaman, in Syria."

And they got furious
and they sprang to their
feet.
He hit them
at their hearts.

> Very many people
> all over the world
> are very good in their families,
> excellent fathers,
> perfect mothers,
> wonderful children,
> but outside of that family circle,
> when facing others:
>> —southerners facing northerners,
>> northerners facing southerners,
>> whites facing blacks,
>> blacks facing whites,
>> Americans facing Russians,
>> Russians facing Americans,
>> Christians facing Muslims,
>> Muslims facing Christians,
>> settlers facing nomads,
>> nomads facing settlers—
> they are hopeless.

And yet,
there will be no peace
and no justice,
no liberation
and no end to exploitation,
until those groups and circles,
those clans and classes
are broken through.

It is often
very difficult
to accept that truth.
It is often
very difficult
to humanize our relations
to that point,
to Jesus' point.
In Nazareth
they said:
"If you don't want us,
if you don't want us
exclusively,
then we don't want you:
fall dead,
perish,
disappear!"
And they marched him
to the brow of the hill
to throw him down
the cliff.
But he escaped,
walking through them,
that time. . . .

11.

JESUS AS HEAD OF THE NEW FAMILY

Luke 5:1–11

Some time ago
there was a short item
in the American magazine
Time.
It was about Africa.
It stated
that an average of sixteen thousand six hundred
Africans
are daily
turning away from their older ways
to be baptized
in Jesus Christ.
A total of six million Africans
do that
every year.
Not all of them are adults,
sixty-five percent of them are babies
or small children,
but thirty-five percent are adults,
that is about six thousand adults
a day.

Theologians,
sociologists,
psychologists,
pastoral workers,
and their research associates
have been bending their learned heads
over these numbers
and they came forward
with very many reasons
and explanations.
But two of the reasons,
explaining all those baptisms,
seem to be
the outstanding ones.
Their first reason has
something to do
with what happened
to Simon
and his companions
in the Gospel
of today.
Simon was a fisherman.
He was a good one,
but no more than that.
He had no time
for the great number of preachers,
Bible-pushers,
and "evangelizers"
roaming through the Palestine
of his time.
He had no objections,
however,
when Jesus asked him
to be allowed to use
his boat.
And again Jesus sat down
—as a real teacher—
and he taught,
while the people were listening
on the shore.

After the preaching
there was no reaction
from Simon.
He does not seem
to have been touched
by the words
of that preacher
at all.
> Jesus asked him
> to bring the boat out.
> Simon thought that
> ridiculous
> and he said so
> in as many words.
> But he complied.
> He put out his nets,
> and at the moment
> that those nets hit the water
>> it was as if
>> the whole lake
>> started to move,
>> because even from the farthest
>> corners and underwater caves
>> fishes swam
>> as fast as they could
>> to be caught
>> by those nets.
Simon had to call others
to get the nets safely
into the boat,
but once those nets were inside,
spilling their catch all over his boat,
Simon
suddenly
realized
what had
happened
and he shouted
at Jesus:

"Get away
from me!
Let me get away
from you!
You are God!
God in my boat!
God in my life!
Oh no, this must mean
my end!"
But Jesus said:
"Don't be afraid,
I am here with you,
be quiet."
And Simon, turned into Peter,
stayed and followed him
very happily.

Many scholars
who studied the relationship
between God and African humanity,
—for instance the well-known
Kenyan scholar, John Mbiti—
found that same idea
Simon expressed.
People in Africa knew
from of old
that they were dependent
on God.
But the knowledge
of that dependence
was also the reason
that
—in general—
people in Africa
did not want
to be too near
to God.

They believed in God,
they prayed to God,
especially in emergencies,

but for the rest:
distance
was kept!
All kinds of stories
are used to explain
that distance.
It is said by some
that in the beginning
God
was very near.
But God moved further and further away
because God could not stand
the pollution
caused by the ever increasing number
of human fires
and their smoke.
Others say
that God could not stand
the human politics,
the endless squibbles
and squabbles.

But,
in the final analysis,
the peoples of Africa,
like Simon,
had the desire
to get God nearer,
to get God as a friend,
as a member of the family.
And that is what God did
when Jesus, his son and our brother,
appeared
among us.
Bwana Yesu
karibu kwetu:
Lord Jesus welcome
in our midst.

"Jesus is the head of this family,
the unseen guest at every meal,
listening in to every conversation."

Another famous African theologian,
Canon Harry Sawyerr
from Sierra Leone,
points in this context
to so many texts in Paul:
>"We are one in Jesus,"
>"We are God's family,"
>"We have God's Spirit,"
>"Christ's blood flows in us,"
>"We are one body,"
>"We are a new family,"
>We are age-mates.

And it is in that way
that we also find
the second reason
why so many Africans
turn to Jesus,
as mentioned in *Time*.
>In Jesus we pass
>the tribal borderlines.
>We come all together
>in him.
>In him
>we form
>one new divine-human family.
>>Alleluia, alleluia. Amen.

12.

PLAIN TALK

Luke 6:17, 20–26

When Jesus gives
his Beatitudes
in Matthew and Mark,
he first climbs a mountain
as if to indicate
that what he is going to say
is as yet
above us:
>an ideal,
>the promised outcome
>of a long climb
>ahead.
When he gives
his Beatitudes
in Luke,
he comes down
from the mountain
into the plain,
at the level
where we live,
and where his listeners
had assembled.

Those listeners had come
from very far,
from all parts of Judea,
from Jerusalem,
from Tyre and Sidon.
They had come,
the Gospel explains,
to hear him
and to be cured.
The people assembled
were people
who had left their homes,
who had left their jobs,
who had left their work,
who had left their worries,
who had left their opportunities
behind.
They had gone
a long way
to hear him
and to be helped
by him.
Then looking
at them,
fixing his eyes
on his disciples,
Jesus says:
"How happy are you
who are poor!
How happy are you
who are hungry!
How happy are you
who weep now!"
What did he mean?
Was he insinuating
that poverty,
poverty with its squalor,
with its bedbugs, lice, and fleas,
with its unavoidable rats,

its prostitution,
child-death,
hunger, starvation,
lack of education,
          sanitation,
          security, and
          vitamins,
tuberculosis, kwashiokor,
and deformation,
makes one
happy?
Did he want to say
that poverty
is desirable?
          Of course not!
          How could he?
          He was,
          on the contrary,
          speaking to people
          and about people
          who were hoping
          to have all that
          changed!
Take the incident
as it stands:
he came down.
While he came down
he saw those hundreds
and maybe thousands
waiting for him.
          What did they come for?
          They came because they hoped
          for a change.
          They came because they wanted
          to see.
          They came because they wanted
          to know.
          They came because they wanted
          to hear.

They came because they considered themselves
as poor,
hungry,
thirsty,
ignorant,
frustrated,
and sad.
They came because they were eager
for a change,
a greater integrity,
a greater human dignity,
a greater justice
and more joy.
And that is why
he praises them
and blesses them,
because those people
considering themselves
in danger and helpless
were (and are!)
the hope
of this world.
They are the ones
willing to listen
to HIM.
There is hope
because of that willingness.
A hope not present
in those who remained home,
thinking that they knew
already,
thinking that they had their fill
already,
thinking that they had their consolation
already,
laughing at any change
or its possibility.
Jesus praised
those who had come,

because they were willing
to listen.
He told them
that if they really would listen
the whole world
was going to change.
A new human alternative
would be realizable.
But he told them also
that very many would be
against those changes.
    That they would be hated,
    accused, driven out,
    and abused,
      denounced as criminals
      and arrested.
But, he added,
be happy
as you are right:
the change will
come.

13.

TEMPTED TO LEAVE THINGS AS THEY ARE

Luke 4:1–13

Last Wednesday
we began Lent.
Very many of you
came to receive the ashes.
We started that day
our commemoration
of Christ's suffering,
his death on the cross,
and his resurrection.
> Those realities
> are definitely essential
> to his life,
> and that is why
> we should be very careful
> in trying to understand
> what happened to him
> really
> and why.
Very many think
that Jesus had to die
because his Father
wanted him to die.

71

His Father wanted to see
his blood
before that parent of us all
was willing
to reconsider
our case.
>Brothers and sisters,
>can you really believe
>that?
>Would it not be possible
>that something
>different,
>totally different,
>happened
>to him?
>A thing that happens
>even nowadays.
>And I think
>that it is not difficult
>to prove that.
On October 29, 1969,
a man died in the United States.
His name was
Clarence Jordan.
This man was a Christian,
highly intelligent,
with two doctorates,
one in theology
and one in agriculture.
>He started a community,
>a mixed one,
>where all kinds of people,
>of all kinds of color
>lived together,
>worked together,
>and ate together.
>They worked out
>an integration
>in the disintegrated America
>of those days.

They lived on a farm
and they were visited one day
by some members of the
Ku Klux Klan,
who came to tell him:
"We are from the Ku Klux Klan
and we don't allow the sun
to set on people
who eat their breakfast
with niggers!"
      Their farm was boycotted,
      they could not buy seeds,
      their roadside shop was blown up,
      their children were shot at
      in the evening hours,
      and several were wounded,
      not hundreds of years ago,
      but a dozen years ago.
Did Clarence Jordan
want that violence?
He did not.
Did he like it?
NO.
He knew that he could stop it
by changing his ways,
by returning to the old patterns.
They told him so:
"Change
and nothing will happen."
They tempted him
to stop;
he refused.
And when Martin Luther King,
the valiant fighter for
human rights,
was arrested in Albany,
Clarence Jordan was arrested
too
and put
in the next cell.

Do you understand
what happened?
Do you see
why he suffered?
Do you realize
why they wanted
to kill him?
Not because of God
in heaven,
but because of the men and women
around him;
because of the old ways,
    the old death,
    evil,
    selfishness,
    power,
    vainglory and pride.
That is why!
Jesus had been baptized
in a queue of people
hoping for a new life,
hoping for a change.
Heaven had not opened
on anyone in that queue before,
nor would it open again
on anyone afterwards.
But when he knelt down,
when the water flowed
over his head,
heaven did open
and that voice was heard:
        "This is my Son,
        my beloved,
        new life,
        new ways,
        new humanity."
And he ran into that desert
to give up
and to forget about
the whole thing.

He had been warned,
death had followed him
from his birth:
    he should have been killed
    as a baby,
    that is why he lived
    for years
    as a refugee in Africa,
    in Egypt,
    and that is why,
    later,
    he even lived in Nazareth,
    all the rest of his life
    as an exile,
    a refugee
    in his own country,
    in his own world.
He had remained hidden.
All publicity had been avoided
after the angels
and that star.
But now that voice
from heaven
had betrayed him.
Now they knew,
everyone knew.
    The devil knew too,
    and he came to tempt him:
    "Give up,
    don't use your power
    in view of anything new.
    Make bread for yourself
    out of stones,
    get rich quick
    as all the others
    did and do!
        Indulge in honor,
        glory, fame, and praise
        as all the others
        did and do!

Rule over the whole world
in the way I,
the devil,
do it
and all the others
did and do!
    Forget about a new start,
    forget about an alternative,
    be realistic,
    be logical,
    be tough,
    and leave things
    as they have been,
    will be,
    and are."
He refused to give in.
He chased the devil away.
And because he refused
he had to suffer
unavoidably.
    Because of that refusal
    he is our only hope
    and if we
    nonviolently
    are like him,
    we too
    will suffer
    in view of the glory
    to come.

14.

HE STARTED TO CHANGE

Luke 9:28–36

It is obvious
from the Gospels
that the people
around Jesus
expected him to do
all kinds of things.
They hoped
that he would change
their situation,
that he would better
the world.
> That was in a way
> even what the devil
> wanted him to do:
>> change the stones
>> of this world
>> into bread,
>> interrupt the laws
>> of gravity
>> and be famous,
>> take over political power
>> and rule as no one
>> ever ruled
>> before.

That is what his disciples
expected him to do.
That is what all his followers
wanted him to do:
>   and they brought their sick,
>   the crippled,
>   the mentally deranged,
>   their children
>   and their worries.

The expectancy
that had been growing
around John the Baptist
was now
concentrating
around him,
to the extent
that they expected
miracles and wonders
left, right,
and center.

In the Gospel of today
he took three of them
aside:
Peter, John, and James.
He told them:
"Come with me.
I will show you something."
And they followed him
excitedly,
very proud of being chosen,
sure of themselves.
He brought them
up that mountain
and,
again,
heaven opened
and Moses was seen
and Elijah.
Their expectations
grew almost wild:

Was the change
going to come?
Were Moses and Elijah
not the great experts
in change and development?
    Was it not Moses
    who had brought his people
    from Egypt into the
    NEW land?
    Was it not Elijah
    who had changed his people
    from an old-fashioned, sinful one
    into a
    GLORIOUS nation?
The three were sure,
it was going to start:
    a totally new world
    with Israel at the top;
    a totally new world
    with rich harvests everywhere;
    a totally new world
    with food for all;
    a totally new world
    with water even more than needed;
    a totally new world
    with plenty of power and energy;
    a totally new world
    with health opportunities and
    social security for everyone;
    a totally new world
        economically wealthy,
        technologically robust
        and politically full of peace,
            love,
            and unity.
And they looked at him
while he was discussing
this changeover,
this pass-over
with Moses and Elijah.

Suddenly
the change
did
start:
>but it was not the grass
>that grew more lush;
>it was not the trees
>that grew bigger fruits;
>it was not the maize
>that increased the size of its cobs,
>it was not the rain
>that fell more abundantly;
>it was not the sun
>that got brighter;
>it was not a further development
>in the field of communications
>and transport
>that changed human life;
>it was not all kinds of buildings
>changing the skylines:
>>IT WAS HE
>>who changed.
>>IT WAS HE
>>who started
>>to shine,
>>HE,
>>the son of humanity,
>>the model of
>>all.

It was in this way
that it was made clear
to them,
those privileged three,
and to us
who read their report,
what should happen to
this world:
>WE,
>HUMANKIND,

SHOULD CHANGE
AND START
TO SHINE.
And while he shone
everything around him
picked up
that shine:
    the grass
    and the trees,
    the mountains
    and their tops,
    the birds
    and the insects,
    Peter,
    John,
    and James.
Again
a voice was heard
and the voice said:
    "Listen to him,"
    do what he suggests,
    change yourself
    according to his model,
    according to his Spirit
        and all the rest
        will follow,
        but do not change
        his priority list.
        Never.

15.

WHY IS NOT EVERY TEAR WIPED AWAY?

Luke 13:1–9

They came to Jesus
with one of the most burning issues,
if not *the* most burning issue,
in the life
of all of us:
> suffering and pain
> and especially the
> suffering and pain
> of us,
> believers,
> those who will good
> in this world.
Pilate,
the colonial military commander,
had ordered
the use of violence
during a riot
in the temple.
Some innocent worshipers,
just bringing in
their sacrificial animals

to appease,
to thank,
to implore,
and to adore
God,
the only one,
the mighty one,
got caught in the melée
and they had fallen
victims
too.
      They had been butchered
      and their blood
      had mingled
      with the blood
      of their sacrifices.
People did not understand
how this was possible.
Just as we do not understand
when we hear
that someone had a car accident
on the way
to church.
      How?
      Why?
         We all face
         sooner or later,
         or all through our lives
         that question
         about suffering,
         especially about the suffering
         of those we think
         to be just.
Why did not God
create a world
without suffering?
a world
where every tear
is wiped
away?

And we forget
that God created
a world without suffering.
It is the world
of the moon,
and the stars,
the sky,
and the sun,
the fire
and our mother earth herself,
the minerals and the
stones.
Next to that world,
painless but also
lifeless,
God created
LIFE
and growth
and interaction.
God did not only want
stones and water and air and fire,
God wanted LIFE,
human life too,
and with that life
    pain
    entered the world:
    food had to be found,
    a tooth had to come through,
    a baby had to be born.
But even that was not all.
God wanted to create
us,
human beings,
in such a way
that we would be ourselves
—notwithstanding our dependency—
the shapers
of our own lot,
real persons.

To realize that
God had to stop
interfering with us
all the time,
even at those moments
that we would go
wrong.
You,
yourself,
do the same
with your children.
At least:
you should do the same.
You love them very much
and because you love them
so much,
you have to free them
from you.
 You cannot bring your son
 to school
 all his life.
 One day he has
 to go alone,
 and you know
 that he might and will
 make a mistake,
 a false step.
You cannot accompany
your daughter
to all the discos
she goes to.
You cannot sit
in a dark corner
of that hall
to watch her
all the time
and every time.
 It is your love
 for him,

it is your love
for her
that asks you
to take those risks.
And mistakes
will be made,
stupid ones
and sinful ones,
selfish ones
and tribal ones,
small ones
and big ones
   and the world
   in which we live
   is the result
   of all those
   mistakes
   next to our
   successes.
But even then,
we might object,
let those who made mistakes,
let those who sinned
suffer,
but not just us,
the just!
   But are we really
   just?
   Aren't we involved
   too?
   Isn't every piece of bread
   we put in our mouth
   a doubtful issue,
   in a world where so many
   are
   without it?
   Is not every piece of pineapple
   out of a tin
   an injustice,

when it is grown and canned
by a multinational
that never pays
any local tax?
Aren't we guilty
too,
when we approach a prostitute,
or when we ruin part
of humankind's genetics
by drinking,
or using bleaching-creams;
when we are involved
in the manufacturing and selling
of useless things;
when we are paying house-rents
that are impossible
for others;
when we contribute
with our tax money
to the world's armaments race?
　　　What is the answer
　　　of Jesus?
　　　He first said:
　　　"Don't think that
　　　any one of you,
　　　he or she,
　　　is innocent.
　　　You are guilty,
　　　all of you."
All of us.
We have all been
negative factors
in the history
of our days.
Positive factors,
yes,
but negative factors
too,
unavoidably.

But then
he said:
"Am not I,
God,
standing on your side?
Am I not participating
in your suffering?
Do I not understand?
Did I not take my part
of humanity's responsibility,
by being with you,
EMMANUEL?
Did I not show you
by my suffering and death,
by my resurrection and glory
that all this
is the birthpangs of a
new humanity
and that it will finally
lead to
victory,
praise the Lord!
A victory of which
each one of you
will be able to say:
"I was a contributing factor,
a real cooperator,"
and then
every tear
will be
wiped away.
Amen.

16.

GIVE ME MY MONEY NOW!

Luke 15:1–3, 11–32

Jesus
was surrounded by people
of whom it is said
that they were seeking
his company.
They were the people
who felt
that they needed him.
Those people
who felt
that they needed him
were
the tax collectors
and the sinners.
> There was a second group
> who kept away from him.
> They were the Pharisees
> and the scribes
> who blamed Jesus
> for being surrounded
> by that first group of
> tax collectors and sinners.

89

And it was then,
confronted with that clash,
that Jesus told
all of them,
both groups,
the group of the so-called sinners
and the group of the so-called just,
a story,
a parable,
to explain himself.

> You know the story.
> You have heard it
> dozens of times.
> It is the story of the
> "prodigal" son.
> The story of that boy
> who went to his father
> and said:
> "I want my money
> now and quick."
> The story of that son,
> the younger one,
> who wanted all he could get
> > —a serious victim of grabbiosis,
> > the grab-grab disease—
> to spend it
> very freely,
> very prodigally
> in order to share in
> the "good life."

> > He went to
> > town
> > and there he spent
> > all he had
> > —the Gospel reports—
> > by profiting to the full
> > from the corrupt situation
> > of that time:
> > > he gambled,
> > > he bribed,

he got drunk,
he bought and paid for
the bodies he wanted,
he led a life of
debauchery.
But then something happened.
There was a drought,
a terrible one.
It did not rain for weeks and weeks,
it did not rain for months and months,
and everyone was feeling
the pinch.
That son too,
he felt like dying,
and,
because of that pinch,
he came to his senses
and said:
"I am dying,
let me go back
and serve my father."
He went back.
Sister or brother,
this is a story
that is repeating itself
all the time.
It is repeating itself
at this moment
in this world
and in this country.
All went well,
plenty of everything.
A coffee boom,
prodigality and plenty
all over:
plus the corruption
that set in
and remained undetected,
because all went well:
tax collectors and sinners,

            exploiters and profiteers,
              sugar-daddies and sugar-mammies,
              gambling and playing,
              bodies sold and bodies bought;
        and then there came
        the great drought,
        no rain,
        heaven remained closed;
        no oil,
        minerals drained away
        and the pinch
        was felt.
And slowly
we are coming back
to our senses.
There are probing committees
everywhere:
            in the civil service,
            in the university,
            in the maize board,
            in the railways,
            in the post office,
            in the hospitals,
            in the insurance world,
            in imports and exports,
        discovering and uncovering
        prodigal sons (and daughters)
        all over,
            we are like a dying generation,
            a dying nation,
            a dying world.
In this time of probing
let us try
to probe ourselves;
how far are we guilty,
co-responsible;
where did we cheat and lie,
bribe and profit,
waste and spoil,

live dangerously
and luxuriously,
where did we brotherize*
and favor?
> And let us then,
> like that prodigal son,
> change our ways
> serving the Father
> and each other.
> If we do this
> we will be received by God
> with open arms
> and we will be brought back
> from death to life.
There remains the question
whether we can do this alone.
Should we not come together
while doing this?
We the sinners
and those others
—the older brother in Jesus' story—
the just.
> That is the point
> of his story.
> What we need is
> a new family,
> a new community,
> brought together again
> around the table
> of the Father.
>> Preaching is not enough,
>> being filled with the Holy Spirit
>> neither.
>> Service to the poor is not enough,
>> political action
>> neither.
>> Prophecy is not enough,
>> resistance to unjust structures
>> neither.

What we need is
that new family,
that new community,
like the one
in the story of
today.

*Brotherize: to promote and favor the members of one's own family only, even when executing a public office.

17.

WHO WILL THROW
THE FIRST STONE?

John 8:1-11

Some weeks ago,
there was a talk over here
at the chaplaincy
about the Gospel of Matthew.
The speaker,
a very learned professor
from Rome,
explained how
the Gospel of Matthew
could be read as
an "apocalyptic" work,
that is to say, as a book
written to console Christians
with the knowledge
that this world,
in which we Christians
seem to be the losers,
will end,
and that in that end
we Christians
will be the winners.

After the talk
a Sister stood up
to ask a question.
She asked:
"I heard what you said.
That is your opinion,
and now you have explained to us
the Gospel by Matthew
like this,
but tomorrow
there will be someone else
with a totally different
interpretation and explanation.
It is all very confusing,
whom should we
believe?"
The speaker gave
in all his learnedness
a rather vague
answer.
But the answer is,
it seems,
that most probably
all different explanations
and interpretations
are somewhere
true.
It is the characteristic
of a real piece of prose or poetry
that it can be interpreted
in all kinds of ways.
A real piece of prose or poetry
is as rich
in its possibilities
as human life
itself.
That is definitely true
of the Gospel text
of today.

It was early in the morning.
He had come to the temple
at daybreak.
He sat down
and started to teach
and to answer questions.
    Suddenly there was a noise
    around the corner.
    A group of excited people
    appeared
    with stones ready
    in their hands.
    They pushed and pulled
    a frightened girl,
    hardly dressed,
    taken straight from her bed,
    where she had been found
    in the dark,
    making love
    with a man.
They pushed her
in his direction.
They made her stand
in full view
of everybody
and then they said:
    "We caught her
    this morning
    in bed with a man;
    we caught her
    this morning
    in the act of adultery.
    Moses has ordered us
    to condemn
    a woman like that one
    over there
    to death.
    What have you
    to say?"

They looked at him,
he bent over to the ground
   —was it to pick up
   a stone?—
they held their breath,
but no,
he only started
to doodle
with his finger
in the sand.
But they,
not giving up,
insisted and persisted
until he looked up
and said:
   "If there is one of you
   who has not sinned,
   let him apply Moses' law
   and throw
   the first stone."
And they started to leave,
the oldest one first,
until no one was left.
   Why?
   Why did they leave?
   What was Jesus' intention?
   There are
   very many
   interpretations
   possible.
Maybe
Jesus wanted to point out
to them,
those men
who had brought that woman,
how hypocritical they were.
They brought him
a woman
accused of
adultery.

Committing adultery
is not something
you can do alone,
just like playing tennis
is not something
you can do alone.
    Where was the man,
    where was the
    second person?
I once asked a group
of students
over here at the university
the same questions,
and one of the lady students
answered:
"He was in that crowd
with a stone
in his hand."
Maybe
Jesus wanted to convince
all those men
(and all of us)
how prejudiced
they were,
blaming the woman
only.
A prejudice
that is going on
all the time.
Leaders in this country,
the political and the religious ones,
are so often "blasting"
the girls,
and only those girls,
for so-called *unwanted* pregnancies,
that you start
getting the impression
that girls can get pregnant
on their own,
virginally.

And when here
at the university
pregnancies are discussed,
then again
there is not a word,
    not a word
about men.
        Maybe
        Jesus wanted to convince them
        and all of us
        that we are sinners too,
        that we should repent
        our sins in matters
        sexual.
Maybe.
But there is also
another possibility.
Maybe
he wanted to say
something
about us
believers.
        He said:
        "Let the one
        without a sin
        throw the first stone."
        So what he said
        really meant:
        let the innocent person,
        let the man of honor,
        let the saint,
        let the man without sin,
        let the man without passion,
        let the man without lust,
        let the holy one,
        let the perfect one,
        let the good one,
        let the righteous one,
        let the faithful one,

let the child of God,
let that one
throw
the first
stone!
How could a sinless one
do a thing like that?
How could a saint
take a stone,
aim,
and hit her
with full force
in the softness
of her face,
of her belly, or
of her breasts?
They understood
and they put their stones
down,
quickly,
without a noise,
carefully,
not wanting to be heard,
and they left
while he went on
doodling with his finger
in that sand.
They moved off,
not because they were sinners
but because they wanted to be seen
as perfect,
and Jesus remained
alone
with her,
and he looked up
and there she was standing
in all her misery
and in all her glory,
and he said:

"Did nobody condemn you?"
and she answered:
"No one, Sir."
    And Jesus,
    the Son of God
    in whom that creature
    there
    in front of him
    had been created,
    said:
        "How could I
        throw a stone
        at you,
        hitting your face,
        hitting your breasts,
        hitting you,
        go away,
        go home
        and be good,
        lead
        a sinless
        life,
        but
        live!"

18.

FROM ALLELUIA
TO CRUCIFY HIM

Luke 19:28–40, 22:14–23: 56

Within a few days
the *alleluias!*
of the beginning of the week
changed into *crucify him!*
at the end of the week.
> How come?
> We could know how come
> as this changeover
> is
> taking place
> also around us
> in our times,
> in our days,
> in our lives.
In 1980
the new archbishop of Canterbury
was enthroned
in a beautiful ceremony,
in splendid splendor,
in a great solemnity,
in grandeur and joy.

He was wearing a mitre
and a cope
on which one of the last
English professionals
capable of working
with gold thread
had been working
for months
and months.
The crowd was enthusiastic:
alleluias!
all over the place
together with the hope
that from now on
everything is going
to change.
In the same week
another archbishop
in El Salvador,
the smallest Latin American republic,
Monsignor Oscar Romero,
was shot,
while saying Mass,
from the back of the church
with a gun
with a silencer.
    You could find a photo
    of his murder
    in all papers.
    In that photo
    you don't see the bishop,
    you see only his footsoles;
    he is flat on the floor
    and a Sister
    next to him
    is praying,
    her mouth wide open
    with shock
    like Mary
    under the cross.

In Canterbury
hope
and ringing bells;
in El Salvador
death
and a blasting
shot.
     In Canterbury
     hope
     that the new archbishop
     will change
     his church,
     his country,
     this world.
In El Salvador
an archbishop
changing his church,
changing his country,
changing this world.
     Hope and
     realization.
     Words and
     deeds.
We all hope,
we say,
but do we really want
our hopes
to be realized in this world,
during our lives?
     We hope that misery
     will be taken away;
     that starvation
     will disappear;
     that thirst
     will be quenched;
     that all people
     may be happy and free;
     we hope that we might live
     a simple,
     a more honest,

a purer
human life:
          but do we want
          all that
          really?
          Is it not
          at the point
          of the possible realization
          of our hope
          that that hope
          is betrayed
          by ourselves?
A political example
from the past
might help
to clarify
what I mean.
          In 1968
          the whole of France
          was full of expectation.
          There was a student revolt,
          a very serious one,
          manifestations
          and demonstrations
          all through Paris,
          day and night.
The students alone
could not change
France.
But they had been in contact
with the trade-union leaders
who always had been speaking
about the necessity of a change,
a needed one,
they said,
a drastic one.
          Together with those unions
          the students might have been
          successful.

According to some
that was the hope,
according to others
that was the danger.
When the students came
to the trade-union headquarters
for the last arrangement
and the final signatures
at the time
appointed for that,
they did not only find the doors
of those headquarters
closed,
but they were welded together
with iron bars
over them.

We should transpose
this example
from a political one into a
religious one.
At the critical moment
over there in Jerusalem
around Jesus
and his alternative,
at the very moment
that the change
seemed
possible,
it was suddenly seen
as a *risk*.
You know what you have,
you don't know what you are going
to get.

The streets emptied.
The doors closed.
The windows got shuttered.
The alleluias
lost their echoes.

A new noise was heard:
"Get away,
we don't want you,
crucify him."
Is that not
what very often
happens
to us
when facing a change
or the possibility
of a
conversion?

19.

HIS FINAL WILL

John 13:1–15

Jesus knew
that his hour had
come.
The hour to pass
from this world
to the Father;
to pass this world on
to the Father.
> He knew,
> they did not know.
> And even he
> in the beginning
> did not think
> so much
> of the end.
> You don't think
> of the end,
> not even at the beginning
> of a *farewell party*.
> There are too many things
> to be taken care of:
> the invitations,

the seating of the guests,
the drinks,
the food,
and the talk,
    but then,
    when the party
    is on the way
    and almost over,
    there is that moment
    that the conversation
    stops,
    the moment
    everybody was afraid of,
    he too.
He knew
that he was going to be betrayed;
he knew
that he was going to be arrested,
he knew
that he was going to be beaten up,
he knew
that he was going to be tortured,
he knew
that he was going to be killed
and crucified
in the middle of the day
on a cross.
    And knowing all this
    he rose
    at the end of the meal
    from his seat.
    They all looked on.
    The conversation stopped.
    They had a fore-feeling:
        Judas
        had left
        in the dark
        of the
        night.

What would he do?
Call them together
for some last admonishing words,
like a dying African father
would do,
speaking to his sons
and daughters?
      What would he do?
      Asking for a paper and a pen
      to write in clear, bold script:
      "I bequeath
      my home
      and my land,
      my cattle
      and my shares. . . ."
He took a bowl
and a jug full of water
and a towel.
He went on his fours
      —with the dogs under the table
      gnashing at the last bones
      of the passover lamb—
and he washed
their feet,
not even looking up,
but washing all of them,
one by one,
thoroughly washing in that way
the feet
of all of us:
      believers and
      unbelievers,
      the old and
      the young,
      the saints and
      the sinners,
      the pimps and
      the streetgirls,

the popes and
the bishops,
the rulers and
the ruled,
the rich and
the poor,
the filled and
the hungry,
the dressed and
the naked,
he washed,
and he washed,
and he washed
without even looking
at whose feet
he was washing
and washing
and washing
and he never intended to stop
because he said:
"Do you understand
what I am doing?
I gave you a model
of what you should do:
wash each other's feet
and after that
break your bread,
sharing it
all over the world,
all over humanity
until
I
will
be
with
you
again
in the kingdom
to come.

20.

DELIVERED INTO
THE HANDS OF MEN

John 18:1–19, 42

John's Gospel
makes it very clear:
Jesus
delivered himself
freely
into the hands of
men.
> When the mob
> came to meet him,
> he asked them:
> "Whom are you looking for?"
> and when they answered:
> "Jesus of
> Nazareth,"
> he made them all
> tumble on their faces
> in the mud
> of the wicked earth
> on which they had been
> standing.

Up to three times
he let them taste
the bitterness of the
earth's lot.
> After that
> he delivered
> himself
> to the corruption
> in their temple,
> to the intrigues
> in their politics,
> to the jealousies
> in their lives,
> to the injustices
> at their courts.

They took him.
They grabbed him.
They detained him.
They interrogated him.
They caned him.
They crowned him
with thorns.
> We took him,
> we grabbed him,
> we detained him,
> we interrogated him,
> we caned him,
> we crowned him
> with thorns,
>> shouting
>> for his end,
>> shouting
>> for his blood,
>> shouting
>> for his death:
>>> *hoping for*
>>> *light,*
>>> *but preferring*
>>> *the dark.*

John's Gospel
makes it
very clear
where this deliverance
into the hands of men
led him.
John makes it
very clear
where the deliverance
of the just,
of those who strive after
righteousness,
into the hands of men
will lead
them.
> You know it.
> I know it.
> We know it.
> What was the end of
> Oscar Romero,
> the archbishop of San Salvador
> in March 1980?
> Where is Martin Luther King,
> where is Mboya,
> where is Pinto,
> where is Kariuki,*
> where are those others
> in their hundreds
> and thousands
> who were shot
> for the sake of justice,
> of an alternative?
It is the evangelist John
who speaks
about the death
of Jesus
in the most explicit way.
> He does not only report
> how Jesus hung on the cross,

how he bled
empty,
how his lungs
collapsed,
how he bent
his head,
how his body
twitched for the last time.
He tells as well
how a soldier
looked up at him
and how he took his spear
and pushed it through
his chest
into his heart
and out flowed
—it is John
who testifies—
his blood
and the last drop
of water.
He was dead,
absolutely and totally
dead.
That soldier
added a full stop
after that glorious
life.
And when they all
went home,
after having killed
—they thought—
all goodness
in this world;
and when they all
went home
after having given up
their most deeply rooted
hope;

and when they all
went home,
convincing each other:
>   "Didn't I tell you,
>   this type of life cannot survive
>   in this our world.
>   Didn't I tell you?
>   Let us forget
>   about it,
>   let us forget
>   about him.
>   Let us be realistic,
>   we have to learn to live the life
>   we have,
>   corrupt and violent,
>   harsh and treacherous."
And when they all
went home,
inasfar as they had homes
in this homeless world,
>   Mary,
>   his mother,
>   and Joseph of Arimathea
>   and Nicodemus
>   and a few others
>   took him down
>   and buried him
>   in a tomb
>   with a stone in front,
>   sealed
>   and blocked.
And the sun
darkened
and the curtains
in the temple ripped
apart
and the whole earth
shook
with vehemence

when it received
his body:
its origin
and
its end.

*Mboya, Pinto, and Kariuki are Kenyan personalities most probably murdered
because of their interest in a more just order.

21.

GOD'S FINAL WORD

Luke 24:1–12

Brother or sister,
we met Jesus
during his last days
surrounded by human beings,
men and women,
boys and girls
like you and me,
> shouting,
> *"Alleluia,"*
> in the beginning
> of this week;
> having a last supper
> with him
> halfway through that week;
> and betraying him,
> shouting,
> *"crucify him"*
> at the end of this very same
> week.
Men and women,
boys and girls
like you and me
surrounded him

worse than a wild pack of
animals,
trying to tear him
to pieces.
And we succeeded:
    HE FELL
    AND DID NOT COME UP
    AGAIN.
Surrounded
and trapped
by all those people
Jesus fought valiantly:
    he tried to answer,
    he tried to overcome,
    he washed their feet,
    he kissed Judas,
    he healed the ear of Malchus,
    he answered Pilate,
    he looked silently at Herod,
    he admonished the women,
    he thanked Simon of Cyrene in Africa,
    he forgave the soldiers,
    he prayed for his murderers,
    he encouraged the robber on the cross,
    next to him,
    from here to there,
        but finally
        he
        bent
        his
        head,
        his heart gave
        up:
            HE FELL
            AND DID NOT COME UP
            AGAIN.
It was and is
as if
we, human beings,

had the last word
in the history
of this man
and consequently
in the history
of all of us.
Wasn't he
our last and only
hope?
>With him
all possible goodness
seemed to have died
in this world.
Today we celebrate
that it was God
who rescued
him,
who brought
him
back to life.
It was God
who validated
him
and his life
and the life
of us,
his people.
The last word
is God's,
and that last word
is not
death,
that word is
life.
>That last word
is not
"NO,"
it is
"YES."

That last word
is not
"We will overcome,"
it is
"We did overcome,"
we
in
him.
     God did not only
     overcome
     the corruption
     around us
     when he raised
     Jesus
     from death.
     He overcame it
     also
     in us:
     God freed him,
     God freed us,
     alleluia,
     alleluia,
     alleluia.
     The old world
     came to an end,
     a new world
     started to live.
Do you reject Satan
and all his works
and all his promises?
With him,
risen from the dead,
we can answer:
     "YES,
     YES,
     YES."
     Amen.

22.

THE HESITATION OF THE TEN

John 20:19–31

That evening
of the first day
of the week
they were sitting together,
because Mary of Magdala
had brought them
that day
her news:
        "I have seen
        him."
They did not believe
what she had told them.
If only
because they did not understand
why they themselves
should not have been
the first ones
to whom
he appeared.
        But nevertheless
        they had come together,
        to wait for him.

Only Thomas
had not turned up.
They were waiting
for Jesus,
they were waiting for his knock
at the door.
That knock
never came.
But he
did.
Suddenly
he stood
in the middle
of them.
They were speechless,
but he spoke
to them,
giving them
his mission.
He said:
       "I am sending you
       into the world
       in the same way
       as I was sent
       into it
       by the Father."
Go into the world
even uninvited,
it needs you;
enter it
without knocking,
without waiting,
whether you are allowed in
or not.
       They looked at him,
       full of doubt,
       afraid,
       unprepared,
       uncommitted,

but he breathed
over them
and he continued:
"Receive the Holy Spirit,
and undo sin."
He left.
They started to speak
all at the same
time.
But they did not do
what he said.
They did not go
out.
They did not undo
sin.
They remained together
talking
though the Spirit
had
come.
Thomas came in,
late,
too late.
They told him
how they had seen him,
how he had eaten with them,
how he had come in
without knocking
straight through the door.
They told him also
how he had sent
them.
They told him
how they had received
the Spirit,
his Spirit
to go out
into the world
to cancel sin.

And it was then
that Thomas
started to
doubt.
>If they had really
>seen him,
>if they had really been sent
>by him,
>if they had really received
>his Spirit and power,
>>why had they not
>>gone?
>>Why had they stayed
>>on the spot?
>>Why had his Spirit
>>not worked?
He told them so.
He said:
"I am sorry,
but I cannot believe
you.
Let me first see
him
for myself.
Let me see
his wounds,
let me touch
his side.
I don't believe
you."
>The Lord
>did come again.
>Thomas
>saw him;
>Thomas
>touched him;
>Thomas
>recognized him;

Thomas
got his mission;
Thomas
got the Spirit;
Thomas said:
"My Lord and my God."
Thomas believed
and with a last look
at his Lord and Master
he went on his way
even all the way
to India.
Brothers and sisters,
let us not compare ourselves only
to Thomas
in this story.
Let us compare ourselves
to the ten others
who did believe
what they saw
but who,
notwithstanding that belief,
did not move
at all.
We might compare
the people around us
to Thomas.
The people who ask
themselves
the same question about us
as Thomas asked
about those ten:
        "If it is really true
        that they saw,
        if it is really true
        that he sent them,
        if it is really true
        that they got his Spirit

to undo
all sin:
    why did they not go,
    why did they not move?
    How can we believe
    the story
    they tell?"

23.

COME AND HAVE BREAKFAST

John 21:1-19

It had been Easter,
but it had not yet been Pentecost.
They had seen him already,
he had given them their mission,
but they had not yet gone.
Things were not yet
sufficiently settled,
things were not yet
clear.
>Peter decided
>to break their indecisiveness.
>He said:
>"Let me go to my work,
>I am going to fish,
>we have to continue to eat."
>And some others,
>six of them, joined.
One of them was Nathanael,
and that is strange.
Did you ever hear
about an apostle
called Nathanael?

You did not,
and the reason is
that he is normally called
with his father's name,
Bartholomew.
Something else
is strange about him
in this report.
John mentions
where he comes from,
from Cana,
and even that does not seem
to be sufficient,
he even adds
from Cana in Galilee.
>It seems that John
>wanted to stress
>that Nathanael
>was not a fisherman at all.
>Cana was not on the lake,
>it was in the middle of Galilee,
>Jesus did not find Nathanael
>on a boat,
>he found him
>under a tree,
>a fig tree.
Nathanael
must have felt
slightly afraid
to step into that rickety boat,
fishing was not his job,
he definitely did not feel at home,
but
—and that is the point—
he joined
because he wanted to be
together with them.
He wanted to be with
Peter.

But that night
they caught nothing.
A disappointment for Peter
but for Nathanael
too.
It became dawn,
the dawn of a new day.
They rowed to the shore
and saw a man standing there
next to a fire.
He asked for some fish
and Peter told him:
"Sorry, no fish,"
and the man said:
"Throw out your net once more
to starboard and you will find
some fish."
That is what they did.
John remained looking
at that man,
and seeing the net crawl with fish,
he looked once more
and then suddenly he understood
and he said:
"It is the Lord."
And Peter almost dropped the net
and he wrapped something around himself
and ran through the waves
to the shore,
and Jesus said:
"Give me some fish,"
and they dragged the net
to the shore
and they gave him the fish,
one out of the
one hundred and fifty-three
they had caught,
and he started to fry it,
and he said:

   "Come
   and have breakfast,"
   and he took his bread
   and he gave it to them,
   and he took the fish
   and handed it round.
We always commemorate
his last supper
and never that first breakfast
after his resurrection
with them.
   That is a pity!
   Suppers are easy,
   they are at the end of the day,
   we are going to rest and to relax,
   we are going to bed,
   everyone is easily kind
   to anyone else,
   husbands to wives,
   parents to children.
   That is why we invite
   each other
   for supper or dinner.
   But breakfast
   is a different issue.
   Supper is most times easy,
   breakfast is very often difficult.
   At breakfast
   we have to start,
   we are still cold and stiff,
   the blood does not yet run,
   and we fear the frustrations
   of the day,
   kindness and gentleness
   have still to build up,
   we need first some coffee
   or tea.
    At the dawn
    of that new day,

at the dawn
after that last supper
and everything that had
happened since,
    Jesus said
    very early in that morning:
    "Come
    and have some breakfast,"
    and they took his bread
    and they took his fish
    and he then asked Peter,
    but not only him,
    all the others too,
    all those who had been
    sitting in that boat:
    "Do you love me,
    do you love me,
    do you love me?"
    And when Peter
    in the name of himself
    but also in the name of his crew,
    that nonfisherman Nathanael included,
    answered:
        "Yes,
        yes,
        yes,"
    he told them:
        "If that is true,
        if you love me
        take care then
        of the small ones,
        feed the big ones
        and you,
        together,
        follow me."
And off they went
following him,
leaving some crusts
and some bones behind,

together with the fish,
the boat
and the now useless
fire,
into
a totally new day
and era.

24.

THE COLD IS OVER

John 10:27–30

John makes a remark
before he reports
the conversation of Jesus
in the temple,
of which the Gospel text
of today
is a part.
>He notes:
>*"It was*
>*winter."*
>John likes to make
>this type of observation
>to depict
>an atmosphere.
When Judas
left the last supper
to betray Jesus,
John notes:
"It was
night."
Darkness had
struck
the world.

It was winter
and cold,
that is why Jesus
did not sit down.
He walked
up and down
in one of the temple corridors
to keep himself
warm.
When it is cold,
life moves more slowly,
people dress more warmly
and are less themselves.
Human relations
cool down,
and it is after having described
that coolness
that John
allows Jesus
to speak.
During this talk
Jesus
is not speaking
like a manager
giving missions
and instructions,
providing the force
and power
to enable us
to do all kinds of
things,
insisting on a good organization
and coordination
among ourselves
of the legacy
he left us.
The mood of the talk,
its tone,
is more intimate
and very personal.

Jesus speaks to them
about his relationships,
his personal relationships
with them.
He calls them
sheep,
but sheep in a very special
way:
>"I know my sheep.
>If I call them they follow me.
>They know my voice.
>I know them by name!"

I know them
by their names.
To some this might
sound
too lofty,
rather far-offish,
highly mystical,
very emotional
and frighteningly personal.
>And that might be
>true,
>we are getting
>almost unrealistically near
>to him,
>but yet
>isn't there the possibility
>that all of us
>might appreciate
>and recognize
>what he really
>wanted to
>express?

Take the issue of those
names:
>"He knows our names,
>he knows your name!"

Some days ago
there was a small item

in the *Daily Nation*
exactly on this point
of the use of names.
It was the story of a reporter
who went
to a reception party
of somebody fairly important.
That rather important personality
greeted that reporter,
known for his hard-coredness,
with his name
and the reporter was so pleased
that he wrote:
     "The greatest guy
     I ever met.
     He knew me by
     my name!"
     You must have noticed
     yourself
     so very often in your life
     the same thing.
     It is horrible
     when somebody
     you appreciate
     and love
     and know very well
     suddenly proves
     to have forgotten
     your name.
You must have noticed
how any human contact
becomes so much more personal
and warm,
in the coldness and
in the winter
of this world,
     if you use
     the name of the person
     you address,
     repeating again and again,

Peter or Mary,
John or Steve.
There are quite a number
of baptisms in this chapel,
last year about six hundred,
and it happens
more and more
that parents ask
when presenting
their children
for baptism:
"Have we to give
this child
a new name
or can it be baptized
with the name we gave
already
in the family,
the child's real name?
Can he be baptized
Otieno,
may she be baptized
Nyambura,
or have we to call the child
John or
Jane?"
Is Jesus
going to call them
with their own names
or with the new ones?
The Gospel of today
seems to be clear
on that.
Jesus
will call all of us
with our own name,
coming as near as possible
to us.
He is not our manager,
he is our brother,

> our friend,
> our relative,
> our age-mate.

Not only that.
He explains
too
that what is true
of him
is also true
of the Father.
The Father too
knows our names,
he too cares for us
like that.

> It sounds romantic,
> but it is a romanticism
> we all know of,
> it is a romanticism
> we all indulge in
> from time to time.

Winter is over,
a new light
has broken through,
relations
are warming up,
we are justified
to sing:

> "He is my shepherd;
> there is nothing
> I shall want."

25.

THE PRICE OF LOVE

John 13:31–35

The Gospel of today
brings us back
to his last supper.
Jesus is at table
with the twelve.
In the beginning of the text
that number is reduced to
eleven
      —Judas left
      in the dark of the night
      to make his last arrangements
      to have Jesus arrested,
      detained and
      killed.
No wonder
that to many of us
that number 11
is still considered
to be
a very unlucky number.
      At the moment that
      Judas left,

141

Jesus started to speak
about *glory*
and *glorification,*
about *love*
and *loving one another.*
Those words:
I LOVE YOU,
are so often heard.
What do they mean?
What does it mean
when a mother
kisses her invalid child
and says:
"I love you"?
What does it mean
when a husband
visits his sick wife
in the hospital
day after day
and says:
"I love you"?
What did it mean
when Jesus
told his disciples
(and us):
"I love you"?
You all know
what it meant,
you all know
the price of love
here on earth;
you all know
what it means
to give life
in a world
that is dying;
it means:
pain,
tears,

crying,
and mourning.
In our common language
we very often
have reduced the meaning
of that life-giving word
LOVE
to a harmless,
    sweet,
    sometimes even sensual feeling
    of goodness,
    and we did that
    not without some
    reason,
    but in the Gospel
    the word
    LOVE
    is always cross-shaped.
When Christ said:
"I love you,"
that cross was included,
the cross was meant.
    When Christ says
    that we should love each other
    as he loved us,
    that love too
    is cross-shaped,
    the cross is meant.
    Did he not say
    that the proof of love
    is being willing to lay down
    one's life
    for the other?
Because of this
we very often refuse
to love.
    We do not help,
    because we do not want
    to be involved,

we do not want
to be hindered.
We refuse the possible,
the unavoidable
tears and pain.
We say
that if you are too good,
you are crazy.
We say
that there is a limit
to everything,
    and rationalizing
    we refuse
    the risks;
    we refuse
    the costs;
    we refuse
    to love
    as he did,
    taking those risks
    and paying those costs.
It is in that sense
too
that we say
that the love of a mother
for her invalid child,
that the love of a husband
for his sick wife,
that the love of Jesus Christ
on the cross,
is something glorious and
victorious.
    It is in that way
    that Jesus' love for us
    is his glory.
    Jesus' love
    for us
    took all the risks involved,
    its price was paid
    very dearly:

in blood,
in sweat,
in tears,
in pain,
and in death.
But once all the pain
would be over,
the price would be paid,
and it was his love
that remained,
just as our love
will remain
in the final outcome,
in the holy city,
when there will be
no tears,
no death,
and no mourning
anymore.
All that will disappear,
but we
in our love
will remain
together
with him,
the one
glorified.

26.

GOING AND COMING

John 14:23–29

This is the last Sunday
before we commemorate
his departure,
before his ascension.
In the Gospel text Jesus
speaks to them.
In a way
he is getting more and more
paradoxical.
He practically seems
to contradict himself.
*"I will go away
and I will come to you."*
>He was speaking
>about the mission
>he was going to give
>to them.
>Almost all the Gospel texts
>of the Sundays between Easter
>and Ascension
>speak about that mission
>of his.

The difference is
that it is now
no longer
his mission
in all those talks
and contacts,
but that it becomes
more and more
the mission of his
followers.
Today
during Mass
the Easter candle
is still burning
in our midst.
The symbol of Jesus Christ,
the light of the world,
easily identifiable,
standing there
burning brightly.
On the coming Ascension day
after having read
how he went up
and disappeared
it will be blown
out.
He will be away.
His fire and his light
left the world,
his power too,
to return to
US
at Pentecost.
Then it will be
our turn
to continue
his task.
He is going away
and he will come.

A paradox
difficult to understand
and difficult
to accept.
        When Pope John Paul II
        was here some time ago
        that same difficulty
        and that same paradox
        became obvious
        in several ways.
There were,
for instance,
those journalists
from all over the world
but from over here as well,
from this country,
very keen,
overkeen,
very critical,
overcritical
to catch
every word
the pope would say
about
corruption,
exploitation,
injustice,
human rights,
mismanagement,
and the transformation of
society,
the more equal distribution of goods,
and so on.
        They were eagerly waiting
        for the words of His Holiness,
        waiting
        as if their task
        as journalists in those issues
        depended
        on quoting him.

It is not only
HE
who got that mission;
it is they,
it is us
also,
and just
as much.
That kind of paradox
became also
obvious
in Uhuru Park
where Pope John Paul II
spoke to the thousands
about corruption.
Those who understood
that word
started to cheer,
just as others had done
in their thousands
some days before
in Kinshasa,
the capital of Zaire,
when John Paul
hinted
at corruption.
    As long as the pope
    spoke about the fact
    that Christians should shun
    corruption,
    everybody cheered
    and yelled
    and approved
    and applauded
    trying to see
    over the shoulders
    in the crowd
    those in front
    supposed to be guilty
    of it:

—in Kinshasa
President Mobutu
left the ceremony
a few minutes later—
but when the pope
went further
and said
that the Christian
who finds corruption
in his country
should ask himself or herself:
"How is this possible?
Didn't I do what I should have done?
Didn't I speak out
where I should have spoken out?
Did I commit a sin of omission?"
suddenly everyone
was silent.
Jesus said:
"I am going away,
but I am coming back.
I played my part,
now it is up to you.
I will not leave you
alone,
I will send my Spirit,
go out
and transform
the world."
The pope addressed
the Kenyan youth,
thousands of them,
at his arrival.
He said:
"I know your dreams";
they cheered.
He said:
*"You should remain faithful
to them";*

they started to sing:
"John Paul Two,
we love you."
He said:
"The norm is that
you should do to others,
what you would like others
to do to you";
they cheered even more
enthusiastically,
waving their banners:
"Totus tuus,"
totally yours.
He said:
"If you remain faithful,
you will succeed,
because with Christ's Spirit,
the power lies in your own
hands";
and they started to sing:
"*He* has the whole world
in his hands."
Once more
the paradox
was clear.
    They sang:
    "It is in his,
    it is in your hands,"
while he had said
what Jesus said:
that the Spirit and the power
is in their,
in our hands!

27.

HANDING OVER

Luke 24:46–53

It must have been
for them
a very difficult day.
And a sad one
too.
　　He had told them
　　that they should be glad
　　for him.
　　"Because,"
　　he said:
　　"I am going home."
　　He told them
　　that they should be glad
　　for themselves too.
　　"Because,"
　　he said:
　　"Now I am sending
　　you."
　　　　It was Chesterton
　　　　who once wrote:
　　　　"The really great man
　　　　is the one who makes others
　　　　feel great."

And another English author,
H.G. Wells, wrote:
"The test of greatness is:
what did the person
leave to grow."
And he added:
"By this test Jesus
stands first."
We don't need those British authors
to know that.
We know it
from our own experience
in life.
We know it
from those moments
that others,
who up to then
had been responsible
for us,
made us responsible
for ourselves.

We know it from the joy
we experienced
when they allowed us
for the first time
to do something
on our own:
a commission,
a message,
a task,
the herding of some sheep,
the care for a baby,
or whatever
it was.
From the beginning
God had done the same:
he made man and woman,
king and queen,
rulers and organizers
in nature.

In Christ God did it
again.
Not only Christ
is going to be
the light of the world;
not only Christ
is going to be
the salt of the earth;
not only Christ
is going to be
the ferment in human life.
We should be
that light,
that salt,
and that yeast.
He said to them:
"Go to the city
and stay
until you are clothed
with the power
from on high."
And they went
to wait
for his Spirit
to come.

28.

THE ONENESS HE WANTED

John 17:20–26

Jesus is away.
The Easter candle
that reminded us
of him
is put aside.
We are,
like the apostles,
in those in-between days,
waiting.
>Those apostles
>must have been waiting
>with a certain apprehension.
>They knew that their waiting
>was a lull
>before the storm,
>a pause
>before their work,
>an intermission
>before their mission.
And it is about that mission
that Jesus speaks
in the Gospel reading
today.

The Gospel by John
speaks again and again
about that mission
left by him.
In John's Gospel
Jesus speaks
twenty-one times
about being sent
by the Father
into this world.
    Today's mission
    is very well known:
    "That they may be one,
    as we are one,
    as you, Father,
    and I, Jesus,
    are one."
We all know that text.
We know it very well.
We know it especially
from an ecumenical context.
    "That they may be one"
    seems to mean
    that Jesus prayed
    that the Lutherans, the Presbyterians,
        the Roman Catholics, the Anglicans,
        the ABC, the AIM, the AIC,
        the SDA, the Legio Mariae,*
        the Calvinists, the Baptists,
        the Methodists and the Reformed churches
    may be
    one.
And yet it might be
that we are wrong.
It might be
that Jesus did not pray
for that unity,
though that unity
will be the outcome
of his prayer.

He prayed
for another unity
among his apostles
and among those
who would listen
to those apostles.
Reducing the text
to "ecumenism"
is, maybe,
one of those attempts
by us
to escape
from our real mission
in this world,
if only because that
ecumenism
is something
that seems to concern
church leadership
and is therefore
the concern of *others*.
We try to escape
all the time
from our real mission.
    Jesus said:
    "That they may be one
    as I am one with you, Father,
    who sent me:
        one in the intention
        to redeem,
        to save,
        to liberate,
        to serve,
        to assist,
        to deliver,
        to make grow.
    Father,
    let them be one
    in that
    redemptive purpose of ours."

It is at that level,
that very practical level,
that Jesus prays
that we should be one.
It is at that level
that Jesus hopes
that the world may start
to believe
in him,
in the Father,
in the Spirit
and in us
his followers.
It is at that level
that Jesus says,
when they report to him
that others are driving out
the devils of this world
in his name,
"Don't bother,
my name is preached,
my mission is on its
way."
Father,
that they may be one
as you and I are one
you who sent me
into this world.
AMEN.

*ABC: African Brotherhood Church; AIM: African Inland Mission; AIC: African Inland Church; SDA: Seventh Day Adventists; Legio Mariae: an independent African church split off from the Catholic church.

29.

IN EXCHANGE FOR
THEIR RELIGIOSITY

John 20:19–23

Up to that fiftieth day
the apostles had been
very pious.
The Gospel tells us
how they went back to Jerusalem
after his ascension,
as Jesus had told them to do.
     The Gospel tells
     that they were seen in the temple
     every day,
     praising
     God their Father
     in heaven
     with their alleluias
     and praise-the-Lords.
The Gospel tells us also
that after that worship
in the temple,
they came together
in that upper room
commemorating Jesus,

159

telling
and retelling
their endless stories
about him
and breaking their bread together
in honor of
him.

> But for the rest
> they did not do
> very much.
> They prayed
> to the Father,
> they commemorated
> the Son,
> but without
> the Spirit
> in them.

Without that Spirit
in them,
nothing much happened
for the rest.
Jerusalem did not notice
them;
the country did not notice
them.

> The corruption in town
> went on
> as normal.
> The towngirls walked
> through the streets
> every evening,
> because they knew
> they would be picked up.
> The streetboys remained
> streetboys,
> the hungry and the exploited
> remained hungry
> and exploited.
> The differences remained
> the differences,

while *they* were praising
the Lord
and commemorating
Jesus Christ.
It was only
at the moment
that the SPIRIT
descended on them
that they
and that everything
started
to change.
    They caught fire,
    divine fire,
    they started to preach,
        to heal,
        to prophesy
        and to change the world.
That is what they did
after having been changed.
What do we do
after the same change?
Are we not living
anachronistically?
Are we not living
as those apostles lived
before Pentecost?
    We adore
    God the Father,
    the first person, we will say,
    in the Blessed Trinity.
    We commemorate Jesus Christ,
    the second person, we will say,
    in the Blessed Trinity.
We say:
"Praise the Lord,"
while our conduct
is no different
from anyone else's
behavior.

We hang a cross
around our necks
and put badges with
"Jesus loves me"
on our T-shirts, coats, and cars,
while we remain,
corrupt,
sinful,
lusty,
and inasfar as Jesus' plans
are concerned
totally
reactionary.
> We praise the Father,
> we love the Son,
> but are we really willing
> to receive their Spirit,
> to change our lives,
> to spiritualize and purify
> our work
> in that fire?
Very many
of us
proudly say:
"Africans are notoriously
religious."
Even bishops say so,
but too gladly
and too often.
Are we really willing
to hand over
our religiosity,
into the hands
of that
Holy Spirit
of God
in us?
> Let us praise
> the Father,

let us honor
the Son,
let us surrender to
the Spirit.
     This country,
     this nation,
     this continent,
     this world,
     needs our life
     in that Spirit
     desperately
     in all ways
     of life!

30.

MEMBER OF THE FAMILY

John 16:12-15

Trinity Sunday
is not an easy feast.
In fact it is an
impossible one.
How would we
be able to know
anything about the life,
and especially about the intimate life,
of God?
We do not even know
so very much of the life,
of the intimate life,
of each other
and ourselves.
> Even that life
> remains hidden
> and unknown.
One thing
every human being
who ever believed in God
knew
is that God
is not alone,

because God created us
next to God.
God must have wanted us;
we could not even think
of ourselves
and our possibilities
before we were
wanted.
Did God want us
because there was so much
loneliness
in the divine life?
> But even if that
> would be the truth
> about us
> and about our existence,
> God's problem was definitely not
> completely solved,
> because humankind
> was totally dependent
> and therefore,
> unavoidably,
> an unequal,
> full of fear
> and awe.
The Jews did not even dare
to give God
a name.
Just as we do not like
to use the name of our boss,
and that is why we call him
boss,
or Mzee,*
or the great man,
or something like that.
> It is not good
> to be too often
> too near
> to those who are
> the boss.

It is not good in your job
to knock on the door
of the office of your manager
too often.
> It is not good at the university
> to knock on the door
> of the chancellor or vice chancellor
> too often.
> He will not even receive you
> and he will warn his secretaries
> against you.
It is not good in a country
to try to see
the president
too often.
And it is in that way
that very many human beings
tried to keep their distance
from God
> by sacrifices,
> by buildings,
> by magic circles,
> by tabernacles,
> by heavy gold studded tabernacle doors,
> by decorations,
> by very many meaningless words,
and in so many African languages,
in so many proverbs and sayings,
it is said again and again:
> don't appeal too often to God,
> don't go too often to God,
> if you can clear your affairs
> without God
> so much the better.
And yet:
> would it not be better
> if God were more
> approachable?
Was it as an answer
to this quest

that God appeared
in Jesus Christ,
who was recognized
as the Son of
God?
>We considered before
>how strange it is
>that so many Africans
>want to be baptized.
>In 1979 alone
>six and a half million.
>Ten years ago statisticians
>expected that there would be
>three hundred and fifty million Christians in Africa
>by the year 2000,
>now they expect
>five hundred million
>by that time.
>Why?
Theologians and sociologists
have been concerning themselves
with that question.
They say
that it is the new bond,
the possibility of becoming
a member of God's household
by baptism
that is attracting
all those neophytes.
>The reason is
>the nearness
>offered in Jesus,
>his protection,
>his brotherhood.
There is even more:
it is nice to sit next to Jesus,
it is nice to be able to appeal to him in need,
it is nice to eat his bread,
it is nice to drink his wine,
it is nice to be able to knock at his door,

but even then
      Jesus is only
      next to us,
      beside you and beside me,
      there is more.
      There is more
      in the Pentecostal
      possibilities opened
      by him
      in us
      through the gift of the
      Holy Spirit.
God is *above* us
      as a star,
      as a parent,
      as a source of life,
      as an ancestor,
      as a chief.
God is *next* to us
      as a brother,
      as an age-mate,
      as a protector,
      as our most important relative
      in Jesus
      next to us.
God is *in* us
      as our new life,
      as our link,
      as our inspiration,
      as our real content,
      the Holy Spirit
      in us.
Just sit down
for a moment.
Just sit down
for a few minutes;
ask yourself
how you relate
to God,

how God relates
to you,
        parent,
        brother,
        and your life
        and Spirit.
Unbelievable
and yet
true:
you are a member of God's
family.

*Mzee: the old one, a term of respect.

31.

THE LEFTOVERS

Luke 9:11–17

It was his last evening
before his arrest.
Judas had got the hint
where he would be
that night.
Judas had left.
  Jesus was sitting with them;
  they had been eating a very good supper,
  not an ordinary one,
  but a solemn one,
  the paschal one
  in which the Jews commemorated
  their rescue
  from Egypt
  and the bondage
  over there.
The bones of the lamb
were still on the table,
just like the rest of the bitter herbs,
a piece of bread
and a jug of wine.

He knew
what was going to happen;
he knew
that he was going to be arrested;
he knew
that he was going to be beaten up;
he knew
that he was going to be killed;
he knew also
why:
he was going to be eliminated
because of his fight
for a different,
an alternative,
a better
world.
He was going to be murdered
because he wanted to eliminate
all those sinful situations
in which his people
were oppressed
and oppressing.
    He could have opted out
    easily;
    if only he would have gone
    to another place
    that night.
    But he had been recognized
    by the others already,
    they knew his secret,
    they knew who he was.
    They had put their hopes already
    in him,
    God
    joining humanity
    in its struggle
    for integrity and
    wholeness.

If he would have opted out
all would have been lost,
hope hopelessly
scattered!
He wanted to give them
a sign,
he wanted to make his intentions
clear,
he had to do it
that night
before his death.
Time was very short,
the table almost empty,
he could only use
what was left over,
and he took the bread
and he took the wine
and he said to them:
"Now listen,"
and while he broke it
he said:
"This is my body
breaking up
to be shared;
this is my blood
being shed
to be shared";
and they ate
and they drank
in order,
as he added:
"To overcome
all sin and alienation
in this world."
Something
you hear very often
over here
at this university
and in this country

is what Dr. William Ochieng*
wrote in the *Sunday Nation*
last Sunday.
He wrote:
>"Christianity
>has been two thousand years with us.
>It got its chance,
>but nothing happened,
>it did not change anything,
>it was too spiritual,
>it did not change any structure,
>it left us
>as we were."

He is not completely right
but he is not completely wrong either.
He made a point:
we are too mystical,
we praise the Lord
but do not share;
we praise the Lord
and pass the person
who is in need,
because we profit
from the existing structures
ourselves.
Christianity is not
a flop;
Christianity has never been
tried out.
Even the sharing
Jesus meant
when he broke his bread
and when he shed his blood
has never been really
tried.
>But how to try
>and where to try
>when you are
>alone?

Jesus did not try alone
either.
He was with those
twelve,
he was with others,
they were together:
>   let us join
>   *together*
>   forming one body,
>   forming his body,
>   and let us
>   share.

*Dr. William Ochieng is a well-known Kenyan historian and columnist.

32.

OVERCOMING THE PAST

Luke 7:36–8:3

The community has to be built,
a community is *due*
to our relationships
with God the Father,
     our Father;
with God the Son,
     our brother;
with God the Holy Spirit,
     our spirit.
A community *due*
also
to the way in which we have
to commemorate him
     by the breaking
     of our bread,
     by the sharing
     of our wine;
     by the breaking
     of his bread,
     by the sharing
     of his wine,

175

by the forming
of his body,
having all
the same blood.
But there is more
to a community
than just that,
and today
one of the other conditions
for any community
in him
is explained.
One of the skills
necessary
to hold any community
together.

Jesus had been invited
to a meal
by a Pharisee
called Simon.
He had accepted,
and while they were
not sitting,
but lying at table,
a girl came in.
We know her name,
Mary of Magdala.
She was a girl from upcountry
who had come to Jerusalem
to make a living.

She was what we would call
here in Nairobi
a towngirl,
which is a nice name
for a prostitute.
At the moment she came in
she had already decided
to change her life,

that is why she had brought with her
one of the main tools of her trade:
all her perfumes.
She had poured them all together
in a jar,
all those gifts she had received
from her lovers,
all the smells and smoothnesses
she had used to attract
her clients.
    She wanted a break,
    she wanted something new,
    she regretted her past,
    and that is why she wept
    over his feet;
    she wanted a break,
    she wanted something new,
    and that is why she kissed
    those feet.
Simon recognized her,
the others at the table
recognized her too,
most probably many of them
had been her customers.
    Simon even recognized
    the smell of the perfumes
    she used,
    and he said to himself:
    "Wouldn't he know
    who she is?
    Would he be so naive
    that he does not recognize
    a prostitute?
    If he was a real prophet
    would he allow
    a thing like this?"
Simon must have been embarrassed
for another reason too.

Jesus might have started to think
that the girl was accustomed
to visit him
in his home,
and that is why Simon
was already making up his mind
to have her thrown out
into the gutter of the street
where she
belonged.
Once a prostitute,
always a prostitute.
　　Jesus read his mind
　　and he did not agree.
　　Jesus read Mary's mind too
　　and he understood
　　how she hoped so very much
　　for a change,
　　　　a total change,
　　　　a different life,
　　　　a totally different life,
　　and he told her:
　　"All is right,
　　your sins are forgiven,
　　your past is forgotten,
　　start anew."
Simon wanted to pin her down
on that past,
Simon would not see
any hope for her,
Simon wanted to fix her
in her sin,
Simon wanted to put her
where she belonged,
Simon refused to see in her
any new possibility.
　　Jesus said:
　　"Forget about the past,
　　start anew!"

This story of today
has something to do
with community-building.
It really has
and we all know this
when we reflect for a moment.
> We only will be able
> to live together
> individually,
> socially,
> nationally,
> and internationally,
> if we take the attitude
> of Jesus.
When a father tells his son:
"Once a thief,
always a thief,"
how can they live together?
> When a mother says
> of her daughter:
> "Once loose,
> always loose,"
> how will they be able
> to relate to each other?
When we pin each other down
on our past,
how can we form
a community?
> Paul writes
> in the second reading of today
> that we should be like Jesus,
> because, says he,
> his Spirit is in us.
> Paul repeats that in his letters
> one hundred and sixty-four times!
> > But that is not the end
> > of Mary's story.
> > She does not just disappear
> > like that,

no,
the Gospel goes on.
It tells how Jesus
went on preaching
through towns and villages.
The twelve followed him,
and that we know but too well,
but some women followed him too,
and that is often conveniently overlooked,
taking care of him,
and one was,
oh, yes,
she was,
that old towngirl
Mary of Magdala,
but now changed,
a new type of
woman.

33.

THE CROSS EVERY DAY

Luke 9:18–24

His cross
is obvious
where Christians
meet,
live,
or are dead.
     That is right.
     Did not Jesus say
     that if we want to be considered
     his followers,
     we have to take
     that cross
     on our shoulders
     every day?
We have heard that
so often,
it seems to be so
well known.
But what does it mean
really?
     I know
     what it formerly
     meant to me.

I know
what I was taught
that it should mean
to me.
Every time something nasty
happened to me,
people around me
would say
that my pain and suffering
were a participation
in the suffering and death
of Jesus Christ:
> that toothache,
> a headache,
> a stomach cramp,
> difficulties in my studies,
> a disappointment,
> a sickness,
> a disaster,
> an accident,
> any suffering.

They said:
that is your part
of his cross,
that is your part
of his suffering.
And some would in this kind of
mysticism
even go so far
as to say:
> "How happy you are
> that you are called
> to suffer,
> God sends his crosses
> only to those
> God loves and trusts."

As a result
you might be tempted
now and then
to shout to God:

"Can you please
stop
loving me!"
        And though it is true
        that in a way
        all human suffering relates
        to him,
        there must be another meaning
        to Jesus' saying
        about that daily cross.
When Jesus spoke about his cross
in Luke's text
today,
the people who listened
did not yet know
that he would die
on the cross.
He knew,
we know now,
but they did not know.
        So he can
        at that point
        not have referred,
        inasfar as they were concerned,
        to the cross
        on which he actually
        would die.
        The cross he referred to
        had something to do
        with the cross
        he was going to die on,
        but it was not
        just
        that cross.
There is another thing.
He told his followers
that they should carry
their crosses *daily*.
But he himself
did not carry the cross

on which he would die
daily at all.
He carried it
at the end of his life,
maybe for an hour or so,
and even then he had to be helped
by that man from an African town
called Cyrene:
Simon.
In fact that cross
carried him longer
than he carried
that cross.

> When speaking about that cross
> they and we have to carry
> every day with him,
> he was not speaking
> about the cross
> you see there above
> the altar only.
> He must have been speaking
> about the cross
> he was carrying
> at the moment
> he spoke:
> the things he was doing
> day by day.
> The things that would eventually
> lead him to the cross of wood
> on which he would
> die.

We know
what those activities
are;
they were his constant
struggle
against *sin*
in all its forms
around him:

the sin and injustice
in the temple service
where some profited
from the piety of the poor;
    the sin and injustice
    in the human relations
    when he defended the adulterous woman
    against her hypocritical oppressors
    and when he told her not to sin
    anymore;
the sin and injustice
in the political field,
in the economic field,
the corruption,
the bribery,
the neglect of children,
the breakup of families
because husbands left their wives
just like that,
and so on and so on.
Name a sin,
call an injustice
and he would be seen struggling
against it
—not violently,
but very powerfully—
every day,
every hour.
    It was in that way
    that he made the enemies
    that would nail him
    on the cross.
    It was in that way
    that he carried
    his cross
    long before his actual death,
    daily.
It is in that way
that we should follow him

by refusing
to be bribed
at the moment
that we could do it,
by refusing to bribe
when we want
something.
>Yesterday I met a mother
>who has a daughter
>studying in Europe.
>One of her friends
>was flying out to Europe,
>and she had cooked some food
>for her daughter.
>She had worked very long
>on it
>and packed it very carefully,
>but at the airport
>a customhouse officer
>told her:
>"You are not allowed to fly
>that present
>out."
They both knew
that this was nonsense.
They both knew
what was expected.
But she told him:
"No,
I am not going to
bribe,"
and the food
stayed here.
>And she is so sad
>about it
>that she can not
>as yet
>eat it herself.

We should not dramatize
a gesture
like that.
But Jesus would definitely
see it
in the light of his struggle,
in the light of his cross.
>That is what he meant
>with his daily
>martyrdom,
>witnessing
>(because that is what
>"martyr" means)
>in your pain
>to the reality
>he stood for,
>and we should stand
>for.

34.

THE LEADERSHIP ISSUE

Matthew 16:13-19

Celebrating Peter and Paul
means celebrating
the leadership
in the early church,
it means celebrating
leadership
as foreseen by
Jesus Christ.
> Peter and Paul
> did not derive their leadership
> from a brilliant personal past.
> Paul was,
> as he himself mentions,
> a murderer.
> He attended the killing of
> Stephen
> and he intended,
> once certified as a kind of
> public prosecutor,
> to kill all Christians.
> Peter was a traitor;

he had followed Jesus
after his arrest
in the court-compound
where he betrayed him
three times
by saying:
"I don't know that
man,"
up to the point
that even the cock
woke up
and shouted
in horror.
Peter and Paul,
both strange characters
to say the least,
and yet
the leaders!
Why
and
how?

Jesus was one day
surrounded by his disciples.
He was on his way
to Jerusalem
where he was going to be
killed.
He knew that,
they knew that.
He had been in hiding
already for several times
and they with him.
They were confused.
They did not see.
He did not correspond
to their expectations.
Nothing is outspoken,
all remains vague.

All seemed strange
in the dark.
They were in that
semi-clarity
in which so much
of our life is passing.
No decisions,
a hand on a naked breast
and the idea:
I should not do this
or should I?
            Then Jesus speaks,
            and he asks:
            "Now listen,
            let us come into
            the clear:
            Who do you say
            I am?"
There are answers.
Those answers betray
their confusion.
They said
that *they* say
that he is
a spirit,
a prophet,
Elijah.
They said
that *they* say
that he is
John the Baptist,
a ghost,
a living dead one.
            But then he speaks up
            again
            and says:
            "Now listen,
            who do *you* say
            I am?"

There is a silence.
No one speaks,
they look at each other,
this is the crisis point,
the knife
on their throat,
the dagger
in their back,
no one speaks.
Peter looks around
and suddenly bursts out:
"You,
you are
the Christ,
the Messiah:
     our hope,
     our model,
     our way out,
     our open door,
     our liberator,
     our Moses,
     our David,
     our life,
     Son of God,
     God!"
He stops,
looking around
for their reactions,
but it is again Jesus
who speaks
and says:
     "Simon,
     thanks,
     you are the leader,
     you are their guide,
     you are the rock."
Why
did he say
that?

Because Peter's word
was a light
in their darkness
and fog,
in their confusion
and doubt.
He made clear
what they
in fear and hesitation
had thought and experienced
all the time.
Now it was
in the open,
now it was
said,
they all sighed
with relief.
The tension
disappeared.
Peter became
the leader
because of his insight,
because of his clarity.
But a leader
how?
It was much later
after his death and resurrection
that Jesus confronted Peter
with that "how?"
Of course
you remember the scene:
"Peter,
do you love me?"
A question in the darkness
of Peter's doubts
about himself:
Peter's doubts
because of his betrayal.

But again
in Peter
the question provokes the answer
notwithstanding the darkness
and the doubt.
Peter answers:
    "Yes,
    you know that I
    love you."
    And (again)
    the clouds disappear,
    the sun starts to shine,
    and it is in that light
    that (again)
    Jesus says:
    "As that is true,
    as I believe you,
    as you love me,
    let your love flow out
    by guiding in that light
    and love
    all things.
    Amen."
What he said
is not only
about Peter
and not only
about Paul,
that preacher
of Christ's love.
It is about
you,
it is about
me,
because we too are so often
called to be leaders
in the situations
in which we live,

creating clarity
where there is
   darkness,
   hunger,
   poverty,
   confusion,
   and despair.
Let us be
leaders,
letting God's love
and our love
flow out
to
all living things.

35.

YOUR NAMES ARE WRITTEN IN HEAVEN

Luke 10:1–12, 17–20

I can imagine
that some of us
might say
that they cannot believe
any more
in the existence of
personified evil spirits
or devils.
But I cannot imagine
that there would be
anyone among us
who would not believe
in the evil
and its force
in this world
in which we live:

      the sin,
      the corruption,
      the unnecessary sicknesses,
      the victims,

the breaking down of relationships,
the lack of trust,
the treachery,
the misery,
the accidents,
the fights,
the wars,
the gossip,
the armaments race,
the atomic warheads,
et cetera.
It is Christ himself
today
who compares all that
with persons
and with animals,
with poisonous snakes,
serpents and scorpions,
and he ordered
those seventy-two
not only to absolve
the effects caused
by that evil;
he ordered them to go
and to squash
it.

We Christians
are very often
very busy
with the struggle
against the evil in ourselves,
and it is definitely necessary
that we squash evil
there.
We confess,
we regret and
we fight against
our own private sins,
our lies,

our lust,
our indecency,
our crudeness,
our bad thoughts,
our evil desires,
our negligence,
our disobedience
and our deceit,
in order to come
    to peace
    in ourselves.
We Christians
have become very interested
in our own inner thoughts,
in our own self-realization,
in the descending into the deepest
abysses of our minds,
in the layers of consciousnesses
we never penetrated before.
We Christians, we talk together
in our prayer groups,
where sometimes
our inmost intimate feelings
are shared
as never before
and listened to
and if possible
glorified.
    But aren't we forgetting
    or overlooking
    that Jesus sent those
    seventy-two
    in their pairs
    not into the world
    of their own souls,
    but that he sent them out
    into the world
    of the towns and
    the villages around?

It is there
that they should
struggle
and chase away,
bringing peace.
   And it is
   only after that
   that they are allowed
   to return.
   It is only after that
   that Jesus assures them
   that they themselves,
   while working out,
   have not been forgotten.
When the seventy-two
returned
they were enthusiastic
about their success.
They had managed well,
evil was undone,
the devil in flight,
justice and peace
did come.
When they told
all this to him,
Jesus said:
"Very nice,
very good,
excellent,
faithful servants,
alleluia,
but your success
should not be the only reason
for your joy.
There is something else:
you yourself
were not forgotten
while you worked,
because of all
you did.

Rejoice
that your names
are written in heaven."
     The peacemakers,
     the merciful,
     the fighters for justice,
     those actively interested
     in human dignity,
     those workers outside,
     those who sometimes
     are called activists,
     will never be forgotten;
     their names
     are written in heaven.
     Rejoice because of
     that.

36.

WHERE IS MAN?

Luke 10:25–37

The Gospel story of today,
the one about the good Samaritan,
is one of the best-known stories.
It is not only so well known
because we all know
that story
from the Gospel.
    It is also well known
    because it is a story
    that belongs
    so very much
    to the life
    of each one of us.
    We all have found ourselves
    so very often
    beaten up and robbed,
    trapped and caught
    alongside
    the outroads
    and the inroads
    of our lives.

And we all have met
so very often
others
in the circumstances
in which that good Samaritan
found his neighbor.
As this story
is so common to us
from so many points of view
let us try
to see it
in a new light.
Let us try
to see it
in the light,
or better,
in the dark
of the question
so many ask
themselves
when something
like what happened to
that robbed man,
happens to them.

It is at those moments,
that we are caught,
that we are hit,
when the first blows
fall over us,
when we are kicked
and robbed,
when we are threatened
and bullied,
that we almost spontaneously
feel and ask
the question:
"God,
where are you?"

Even Jesus asked
that very same question
over and over again
when hanging on the cross:
"My God, my God,
why have you
forsaken
me?"
         That question
         is heard
         all over the world
         where there is
         torture and cruelty,
         discrimination and misery,
         negligence and stupidity.
It was a question
that was heard so much
on the battlefields
and in the concentration camps
of the Second World War
and in all the wars
and camps
thereafter
that it keeps ringing
in the ears and hearts
of all of us.
         To give only one example,
         an example from a book
         called
         Sophie's Choice.
         It is about a mother
         in the Polish town Krakow
         who was arrested
         because she smuggled
         some meat to her sick father.
         She was arrested
         with her two children,
         a boy of seven called Jan
         and a girl of four called Eve.

They were transported
in a train
to a camp.
The children were
very upset
to be packed so tightly
with all the others.
Sophie knew
where she was going,
she knew what was going
to happen:
there would be a selection
at the end of the trip,
one line chosen to work,
a second line chosen to die.
They arrived
after five days.
They had to queue up
in front of a doctor.
She stood in the queue,
her turn came,
she got frightened,
she addressed the doctor,
a young man in a uniform,
and she said:
"I believe in God,
I believe in Jesus,
in their name
please let me keep
my children."
He said:
"You believe in God,
you believe in Jesus,
but did Jesus not say,
'Let the children
come to me'?"
And then he said:
"You may keep one
of your children with you.

The other one will have
to go;
which one
do you choose?"
She said:
"You mean
I have to choose?"
He said:
"Yes,
that is the privilege
I grant.
Choose!"
Sophie shouted:
"But I cannot
choose,
Let me not
choose!"
He said:
"Make your choice;
if you don't
I will send both of them
over there!"
      She chose,
      she chose the boy,
      Jan,
      and saw her daughter
      disappear.
      Where was God
      at that moment?
      Where was God
      at that time?
      Where is God
      at all those moments?
      Where is God
      now?
There was that man
traveling from Jerusalem to Jericho.
He must have been doing business,
he must have been scared,

he passed a bush
or he was in the bend of the road
when they came.
He shouted
and he pleaded
to no avail.
They beat him up,
they took everything he had
and disappeared,
leaving him for dead
alongside the road,
half-conscious.
>And he too
>started to plead:
>"God,
>where are you?"
>"God,
>where were you?"
A priest
passed,
a Levite
passed,
a Samaritan
stopped.
>He had asked:
>"God,
>where are you?"
>and that Samaritan
>stopped,
>moved by his pity
>for the life
>of that man.
>>*The question*
>>*was answered.*
>>The question:
>>Where is God?
>>is the question:
>>Where is man?
>>Where is man?

The story about
the good Samaritan
is not only a story
about
who is my neighbor;
it is also a story about
how we experience
God,
      when we are in need
      of God,
      when others are in need
      of God.
It is at the moments
of mercy
that God shows.
It is at the moments
that we allow God
to be with
us.

37.

MARY'S EXTRA

Luke 10:38–42

Jesus arrived in Bethany.
He had been threatened already.
He had been hiding already.
He had been interrogated
by the security forces already.
He was not welcome everywhere
anymore.
The law-abiding citizens
started to shun him.
When he entered Bethany
very many doors and windows
closed.
Children were called
home
and their parents watched
him
from behind the curtains.
     But Martha came
     out of her house
     to meet him,
     she welcomed him,

she made him sit down,
she washed his feet,
she offered water to wash his hands,
she gave him a drink,
she said:
"You are so welcome."
And Jesus sat down,
and he took his drink,
and he was so happy
to be for a moment
at a home.
And Martha went to the kitchen,
and she brought out the food;
there was the noise of pots and pans,
the smell of the baking of bread,
the perfume of fruits and vegetables and wine,
the noise of boiling water
on the fire,
very homely,
very pleasant
with the cat
purring
in a corner.

> Martha was very busy
> and so was her sister Mary.
> They both wanted to receive Jesus
> as well as possible.
> They both were like good Samaritans
> to him.

But Mary did more
than that;
she did not only serve
and help.
According to the original manuscripts
(with the exception of one version only)
Mary
also
sat down at his feet.

In the translation that is used
for our reading today,
that word "also" is missing,
but it really should have been
there.
Martha was busy,
Mary too,
but Mary did that extra.
Martha was like the good Samaritan,
so was Mary,
but Mary did more.
    And Jesus let both
    go their way.
    He appreciated Martha
    and her running
    up and down
    to the kitchen.
    That running was definitely
    a sign of her love
    for him,
    and of her faith and
    hope.
Martha is doubtlessly
part of him,
but when Martha
starts to condemn
her sister
for not helping her
in the serving
and for sitting at
his feet,
he speaks out and says,
that Mary was right
in listening to him,
in listening to the Lord,
in listening to God.
    We all should resemble
    the good Samaritan,

but we should not forget
that the story about him
was preceded by the saying:
"You must love the Lord
with all your heart,
with all your soul,
with all your strength,
and with all your mind,
and your neighbor as yourself."
We should all
follow the example
of Mary,
with the extra she added
to what Martha did
whom we should follow
too.
To have faith
means
to come down from the donkey
of your ordinary life,
to help others,
to demonstrate and protest,
to work and to study
in their favor.
But it means
also
to listen to the Lord,
to pray and be attentive
so that we can *monitor*
all our service
in the direction
of his kingdom to come.
We have to serve
our neighbor,
we have to listen
to the Lord.
We have not sufficient
Marthas among us,

but they are certainly
more numerous
than the Marys
and that is not only
a pity,
it is something
that is felt.

38.

HIS PRAYER AS THEIR FEEDBACK

Luke 11:1-13

Mary was sitting
at the feet of the Master.
She was listening
to what he had to say.
>Listening is important,
>listening is the start,
>listening is not passive;
>by listening
>our mind
>is built
>and our heart
>fills up.
>Listening is
>receiving,
>listening is
>absorbing,
>listening is
>registering,
>but listening is not
>all.

His disciples
had been listening
for days and days,
for weeks and weeks,
in the morning,
in the afternoon,
in the evening,
and during the night.
The time had come
to speak.
It is in our words
that our hearts
and our minds
express and
find themselves.
> We know nothing about
> ourselves,
> about what
> is hidden in us
> until we speak.
> We know nothing about
> each other,
> about what
> is hidden in us
> until we speak.
>> And then
>> word by word,
>> phrase by phrase,
>> we discover ourselves
>> and the others.
That is why a person's
first words
are so important,
but his last words
too.
The whole family
rejoices
at the first word
of a baby,

but the whole family
assembles
also
to hear
the last words
of a dying family member.
>How should they pray,
>how should they speak to God
>after having heard
>all he had told them?
How should the echo
of his words,
bouncing back
from the deep pits of the hearts,
sound?
They did not know
so they went to ask,
and that question
in itself
was already
their first attempt
to pray:
"Lord,
teach us
how we should pray!"
He looked up
from his own prayer
and he said:
"Do it like this:
say:
>Our Father,
>who art in heaven,
>hallowed be they name,
>thy kingdom come,
>thy will be done
>on earth
>as it is in heaven.
>Give us this day
>our daily bread

and forgive us our trespasses
as we forgive
those who trespass
against us.
And lead us not
into temptation."
It was in that way
that they suddenly
discovered in themselves
God
as a Father
with a will
that should be done
not only up there
but down here
in assuring bread
for all,
which means
bread that is
shared
every day.
It meant
also
that the past,
in which that bread was not shared,
should be forgotten
and forgiven
by ourselves
as it will be forgiven
and forgotten
by that Father
who will gladly receive
any son or daughter
coming back
home.
        And to prevent
        that ever,
                ever,
                ever

that unsharedness
would start again
   in racism,
   in exploitation,
   in neo-colonialism,
   in discrimination,
   in apartheid,
   in trade-barriers
   or anything like that
they heard him
and themselves
pray:
   "Lead us never
   into that temptation
   anymore."
The prayer
was over,
the AMEN was said:
heaven lay open,
so lay the earth,
a brotherhood was formed
the sisterhood confirmed,
sins were forgiven
and bread
was assured.
   They looked at each other
   with new eyes
   because of their new hearts.
   So that is who we are,
   that is how we are.
   Let it be,
   let it be.
   Amen.

39.

MONEY AND THE KINGDOM OF GOD

Luke 12:13–21

During these Sundays after
the descent of the Holy Spirit
many aspects of human life
are gradually seen
in the light of
the kingdom to come.
Today the theme is money.
Money.
A man came to Jesus;
he had only one question,
a question about money.
He asked him:
"How do I get it?"
"I have a right to it,"
he said,
"Please, Jesus, help me,"
he asked,
just as so many of us
would pray to him
asking for money.

Answering him,
Jesus does not even refer
to his question:
"How do I get it?"
Jesus speaks about something else
as he does so very often
when asked questions.
Our questions
do not often seem
to be the best ones.
> He does not speak
> about how to get money.
> He does not speak
> about how to use money
> in order to get more of it.
> He speaks about
> how to use it
> to become rich
> in the sight of God.
> He told them
> the story about that
> upcountry man
> who got an enormous harvest
> and who built a large barn
> to hoard it,
> for himself alone.
> He called that man
> not clever
> —as we might do—
> but a fool,
> not because he was unjust,
> but because he was plain stupid,
> thinking of himself
> alone.
I just spent one week in Europe.
There were some study-weeks,
and the subject of the conference was
what to do as a Christian
in this world.

There were very many people
in town,
as those study-weeks coincided
with some cultural festivities.
The almost ten thousand hotel beds
were all reserved,
there were concerts every evening
and even during the day,
the shops were full
and so were the streets,
the weather was fine,
nobody seemed to be hungry,
everybody looked well dressed
and yet
during the discussions
it was obvious
that everyone was upset
and worrying
not only about a possible war,
but about
the lives
they are living:
"It cannot go on
like this,"
"We have no
contacts,"
everyone only thinks
of himself,
of herself.
All we can talk about is
money,
and the things you can buy for
money.
    Hardly any children
    left,
    only dogs,
    not big ones
    but small ones,
    poodles.

A student from Poonah
in India
came to me
and he said:
"I am desperate,
I am a Christian,
but there is no Christianity here,
churches, yes,
sung High Masses, yes,
choirs, yes,
liturgical rules, yes,
communion, yes,
but hospitality,
   community,
   understanding,
   no!"
The conference had invited
me to speak about African Christianity;
there had been someone from Japan
and from India
to speak
about alternative lifestyles.
There were Europeans also
who spoke about
Taizé and other new community
efforts.
   The audience
   was very interested
   in all those developments,
   because the audience
   was in general
   desperately looking for
   what to do
   with their lives,
   what to do
   with their wealth,
   what to do
   with their talents,
   what to do
   with their money.

That day Jesus
faced that question.
His interrogator
was only one
out of the multitude
having those same
questions.
        He had a message
        about money.
        At his birth
        his own mother
        had sung
        an economic hymn:
            the hungry will be filled,
            the rich will be sent away.
        He himself had spoken
        very often about money
        and property rights before:
            blessed are the poor,
            give to those who ask,
            leave all things and follow me,
            take nothing for your journey,
            sell what you possess.
Today,
facing his questioner
he gives us
his most fundamental advice
on how to use
our money.
He said:
"Use it
making yourself rich
in the sight of
God!"
        Use it
        in a kingdom context,
        use it
        for human life,
        use it
        to make your life

and the lives of others
healthy and sound.
Use it
for what you need,
and if there is anything left,
use it
for what others really need
and yet lack,
use it
in view of human life,
its health and its strength
only,
because the glory of God
is that kingdom of God
here on earth:
HUMANITY
ALIVE!

40.

THE GREAT DEAL
GIVEN TO US

Luke 12:32–48

It is examination time.
The end of the academic year
is very near.
    Some have been growing
    visibly thinner;
    some changed their color
    considerably,
    there is more tension,
    friends accuse each other
    of being informers,
    tempers are often high,
    and all the conversations
    you can overhear
    while passing in corridors
    are about
    how percentages are
    counted up,
    how averages are
    determined,

and how one lecturer
(hopefully)
marks less strictly
than another one.
All this means also
that in a few days' time
many of you
are going to leave us
with your new specializations,
with your new talents:
>   *engineers,*
>   though they never built
>   a house;
>   *lawyers,*
>   though they never defended
>   anyone;
>   *specialists in literature,*
>   though they still have to write
>   their first line of
>   poetry or prose.
>>   They are going to leave us,
>>   you are going to leave us,
>>   to find a place
>>   and a job
>>   in society.
What do you hope
to obtain
through that job;
what do you really
want to do;
how are you going
to relate to others;
what are you going to use
your skills
and even yourself,
your own personality,
your gifts
and your talents
for?

To enter the rat-race,
the man-eat-man society,
to get rich
and affluent
as quickly as you can manage,
to become famous
or notorious?
In the Gospel reading of today
Jesus gives
his answer
to those questions.
He obviously
considers us
from the divine point of view,
and in that view
we are put in this world
as God's investments
in human life.
    We are put in this world
    not as owners
    of the world
    or of each other
    but as servants,
    to whom this world,
    to whom the others,
    to whom our own lives
    are entrusted
        and that life
        and those gifts
        and our skills
        and our specializations
        and our talents
        are given to us
        in trust,
        so that we give others
        every season
        their measure of wheat,
        or to say it less concretely:
        all they need.

It is a view
in which
we all should
be aware
that we are not the proprietors,
that we are not the masters,
that we are not put over others,
that we should not eat and drink,
or overeat and overdrink
on our own.
It is a view
in which
we should serve each other,
sharing and participating
in what we are and have
together.
          Mind you,
          this is not only true
          of your skills
          and professions,
          it is also true
          of yourself,
               of your heart
               and all its possibilities
               of tenderness, compassion, love,
               and consoling power;
               of your imagination
               with its possibilities
               of understanding, empathy,
               and sympathy;
               of your body
               with its possibilities
               of help and support,
               of holding each other,
               of work and bringing forth
               children;
          it is also true
          of your traditions
          and politeness,

of your communalism
and its interpersonal relationships,
your culture,
the dancing and
your art.
    It will be difficult
    to realize
    these ideals
    in the world
    you enter
    and are already part of.
Ex-students who left before you
will say
that it is almost impossible,
that they feel isolated
and lost,
that the ideals of our community
over here
in Jesus Christ
are overrun
by other things.
    We should organize ourselves
    better
    and keep contact
    as a small flock,
    that life-unit
    of which Jesus himself said
    in the beginning of the reading
    of today:
        "There is no need
        to be afraid,
        little flock,
        for it has pleased
        your Father
        to give you
        the kingdom."
        And that is
        how it
        will be.

41.

HIS KIND OF PEACE

Luke 12:49–53

The problem
in the three readings
for this Sunday is
evil.
     In the first reading
     Jeremiah
     is put
     in a well,
     very deep down,
     cut off from the light,
     up to his knees
     or maybe even up to his elbows
     in the mud
     because he fought
     in his town
     against sin
     and evil.
In the second reading
we are asked
not to cling to evil
but to stick to goodness,
to fight the battle
till the end.

228

And in the Gospel
Jesus says:
"I came to bring
a fire,
a purifier,
and a new Spirit!
I did not come to bring
peace
but division,
dissent,
and war!"
Strange texts,
strange to us
who are accustomed
to depict Jesus
beautifully
with large eyes
and a shapely beard,
in soft colors,
beautifully dressed,
with a sweet glow
all over him.
The warning today
is clear.
He says:
"Don't think that I came
to bring
an easy peace.
I came to bring peace,
yes,
but I did not come
to pull wool
over the misery
in this world
so that nobody can see
it anymore.
Don't think that I came
to pull a blanket
over all the coldness
of human relations

so that the shiverings
will no longer be felt.
No,
I did not come to bring
that peace.
I came to bring a fight,
a battle,
a fire,
a sword,
to undo all the evil
in this world.
And you,
you should join
in my fight
against that evil,
against that sin."
We can join that fight
in very many ways,
by our confessions
which we should not only see
as occasions to ask for forgiveness
and to make up
for the past
but also as a means
to combat
and to overcome
sin
in us.
We can join that fight
by educating our children
well,
by counseling
and correcting the people
we live with.
We can join that fight
by insisting on honesty
and fair deals.
But there is more
to that fight,
to that fire,

and to that sword
than only sin.
The University of Nairobi
is a very interesting place
and strange things happen
every day.
One of those strange things
happened to me
some days ago.
I was walking
through the campus
when suddenly
one of you,
a student,
carrying some files and papers
under his arm
(showing to himself and to others
that he was busy studying)
rushed up to me
in one enormous swoop.
He stopped me
and said:
"Can I ask you
a question?"
I answered:
"But you are doing that
already;
what is your second
question?"
He said:
"Why do you mention
before you wash your hands
during Mass
sin and *iniquity*?
What is the
difference?"
I am afraid
that my answer
at that moment
was not very clear.

It was too quick.
It was too
unexpected.
Why that double-up
when speaking
about evil:
sin
and
iniquity?
There is a difference.
Sin is not the only evil
that terrorizes
this world.
There are other things
for which nobody
seems to be responsible:
our sick political systems,
the armaments race,
our competitive educational system,
the multinational exploitation,
our difference between the rich and the poor,
the bureaucratic setup of administration,
our industrial relations,
the world's economic order,
evil for which nobody
seems to be personally
responsible.
An evil that is like
witchcraft
that bewitched
so much in our world.
Brothers and sisters,
when we join Jesus
in his invitation
of today
we are facing
a very great and
a very necessary mission
indeed.

That iniquity too
has to be overcome!
Alone
we can do nothing,
but together
        and with the fire
        he brought,
        the fire of the Spirit,
        we can purify
        and cauterize
        this whole wide
        world.

42.

A NARROW DOOR IS A DOOR

Luke 13:22–30

A narrow door is,
of course,
a door.
It can be passed through,
otherwise it would not be
a door.
>The narrow door Jesus speaks about
>is not only the door
>into life
>over there,
>but also to life
>over here.
>To be saved
>is not only a question
>for the hereafter,
>but also
>for the here and now.
That narrow door
is the life-promising
door.
Just as the narrow path
is the life-promising
path.

It is an "eye-of-the-needle"
situation we all have to go through
in order to
live.
> A richly laden camel
> cannot pass,
> and when we load ourselves
> with riches
> as if
> we are
> animals of burden
> we won't make it either.

The reason is not difficult
to guess.
Jesus did not use the word.
The word as such
most probably
did not even exist.
But Jesus spoke
about
what we now call
alienation.
> A human being
> that goes through life
> like a camel,
> transporting on its back
> and along its flanks
> a rich load of all kinds of goods,
> is not going to creep
> through the eye of the needle
> when trying to make its passage
> into life.

That human being
is no real human being
anymore.
He or she
is not
himself or herself.
Such a human being is,
> because of that load,

because of that attitude,
because of that disposition,
a stranger
to himself or to herself,
an alienated creature.
One that missed
its purpose,
its chance,
its nature,
and its life.
    A famous English author
    wrote a book,
    a parable
    that runs somewhat parallel
    to the Gospel of today
    on that narrow path,
    on that narrow door,
    on that eye-of-the-needle story.
    Graham Greene
    called his book
    Doctor Fischer from Geneva
    or
    the Bomb Party.
        In that book
        an enormously rich man
        tries to fish out
        (his name is "fisher")
        what people are prepared to do
        for money.
    To find out
    he organizes parties.
    The guests at his parties,
    all very rich people too,
    get after the parties
    a very expensive present.
    But,
    there are two conditions
    to each party
    and to each present:

the guests are not allowed
to contradict Dr. Fischer
and they have to eat
what he offers them.
There are several parties,
and each time
Dr. Fischer
goes further in his
tests.
    In one of the last parties
    he offers his guests
    —while he is eating
    all kinds of delicacies—
    cold
    saltless and sugarless
    porridge.
    They eat the disgusting
    porridge,
    they eat at the command of Fischer
    a second,
    a third helping,
    though it makes them
    sick.
They eat
in view of the
presents.
    And then there is that last party,
    the final test,
    the *bomb party*.
    There are seven guests,
    the food is good,
    there are no presents,
    but there is a barrel
    with sawdust.
Dr. Fischer explains
that there are seven Christmas-crackers
in the sawdust of that barrel.
He tells them
that in six of those crackers

there are checks for
two million Swiss francs
each,
but in the seventh cracker,
he explains,
there is a lethal bomb,
that will blast the person
who "cracks" it
into the air
for ever and ever.
    But all the guests
    with one exception
    take the risk
    to be blown
    into the air
    forever and ever
    in view
    of the possibility of
    getting
    money.
Your money
or
your life.
They prefer the money
to their life.
    And throughout
    the Gospel reading of today
    Jesus insists:
    prefer your life,
    prefer life
    to anything else.
    Don't be like
    a richly laden camel;
    don't walk the
    wide road
    where you are going to lose
    yourself.
    Pick the
    narrow one,

the lifeline
leading to the kingdom,
the royal kingdom
of
real
life,
creeping through
the eye of the needle
to be safe
and
saved.

43.

GOD'S DYNAMISM

Luke 14:1, 7–14

The Gospel reading today
is at first sight
rather down to earth.
  It seems to give
  an answer
  to the question
  how to behave at table,
  how to behave at a party.
You should not just walk over
to take the best place:
information
that might have been very useful
for the companions of Jesus
when they went
for their first time
to a dinner
in the house of a leading
and rich,
sophisticated Pharisee.
  Those companions of Jesus
  were very simple fishermen

and most probably
they did not know
how you are supposed to behave
at such a dinner.
I would not be surprised
if Peter
had walked up
to the best place
straightaway.
   You should not just walk over
   to take the best place.
   It is the type of advice
   that parents give so many times
   to their children.
   It is the advice that friends
   give so very often to friends:
      don't sit in the best place
      just like that,
      because if you do that
      you might be sent away from it,
      you might be sitting
      in the place of the host
      or of his guest of honor:
      the permanent secretary of higher education
      or somebody like that.
   And if you are sent away,
   if you have to stand up,
   there will be laughter,
   embarrassment,
   and a lot of sniggering.
It is advice
that is even given
in another place in the Bible,
in the Old Testament,
Proverbs 25:6.
There the advice reads:
   "Do not put yourself
   where the great are standing,
   it is better to be invited:

'Come up here'
than to be humiliated in front
of all the others."
And in an explanation of that text,
or better, in a commentary
that was already known in the time of Jesus,
some Rabbis even suggested
that when you go to a dinner
or a party
or a meeting
you always should take
three places below the place
you are supposed to be.
Three places too low,
waiting for someone to come to you
to say:
"Don't sit there
come higher up."
    All this had nothing to do
    with *humility*;
    it had all to do
    with human politics,
    with human wisdom,
    with human cunning,
    and even with sharp foresight.
        Because
        if you really would have taken a place
        too high for you,
        and if the important person
        whose place it was,
        would come in late
            —and important people almost always
                come late
                to show how important
                they think themselves to be—
        you might lose your place
        at a moment
        that all the other places
        are occupied already,

and you might not find any place at all
and you would have to stand in a corner
for the rest of the party
or you would just have to leave.
But do you think
that at that occasion
Jesus only taught them
how to avoid embarrassment?
I wonder.
I don't say that Jesus
never gave
that type of advice.
He might have told his companions
now and then
how to behave,
to comb their hair
or to polish their shoes,
but I think that the text of today
digs deeper
because in the end
of the story
he tells us
how we should behave
when we invite people
to share in our lives:
　　what kind of people we should invite,
　　not the rich and the influential ones,
　　not the big fish and the *magendo mafia,**
　　but the poor and the crippled,
　　the orphans and the widows.
And even Luke himself,
the reporter of this story,
does not seem to believe
that it was a piece of advice on politeness
only.
He calls Jesus' advice
a parable,
a story with a further meaning,
a story with a double bottom.

The question Jesus answered
was not so much on
how to behave at table.
It was an answer to the question
how we should live our lives.
The question was not
politeness
but
Godliness.
The question is not
where should I sit at table,
but
how should I live?
And as you all know,
dear brothers and sisters,
that is a very much asked question
in this country,
in this university.
That question may take all kinds of forms:
—what should I do to be saved?
—how can I be like Christ?
—how can I be sure that I walk his way?
—what does it mean to live under the influence
of God's Spirit?
How can we check,
or measure,
or discover,
or discern,
or control
the movements of the Spirit of God
in us?
It is to those questions
that Jesus seems to give an answer
in this parable.
The meal,
the banquet,
he speaks about
is God's banquet,

it is the dinner
in which we,
all who live,
are participating.
Every one of us
who is alive
is invited by God
in this feast of our lives.
We are all gathered around
that dish called human life,
God's gift to us.
>But we are sitting
>in different places.
>Some are profiting from this life,
>God's gift,
>to the full
>and even more.
>They are rich and important,
>honored and well fed,
>owning beautiful houses,
>surrounded by hundreds of things.
>But others are sitting in very low places,
>they hardly can enjoy the meal,
>they have insufficient or nothing
>to eat,
>they are thirsty or in prison
>for nothing,
>they are worried and scared.
And the parable of today
tells us what the host,
what our host God
is going to do
about them.
The parable of today
indicates the nature of God's movement,
of God's tactics and God's strategy
at the table of life,
it reveals to us God's dynamism.

It tells us
how God goes to the poor
and the wretched and the lowly placed ones;
it tells us
how God moves them up.
That is God's movement,
to make the poor move up.
That is why God is called
    the Father of the poor,
      the Defender of the widows,
      the Protector of the orphans.
That is the movement
God started again and again
in his world,
in its history:
    think of Moses,
    who rescued and moved up the oppressed Jews;
    think of Mary,
    when her womb was filled with Jesus,
    and who shouted:
    "God did not come to the important ones,
    he came to me,
    barely seventeen,
    in a village
    totally unknown.
    God exalted ME and in me
    all those like ME."
That movement is
GOD'S DYNAMISM
in this world
    and it should be
    our dynamism too.
If we are of God,
if you are of God,
if we want to test our lives,
if you want to test your life,
if we want to check whether the Spirit is in us,
if you want to check whether the Spirit is in you,

this is the norm,
that is the test:
> are you living in such a way
> that you help those
> who are underprivileged
> to move up,
> are you living in such a way
> that you enter into the movement
> God introduced
> into this world?

And don't say
that this applies to others,
it applies to all of us
and we can,
all of us,
help in that movement
in a thousand different ways.
> It will, of course, also be
> the test at the end of our history
> when we all will stand before
> Jesus Christ;
> when we all will be facing
> our last examination questions,
> our last test,
> not a written one
> but an oral one,
> > when he will ask us,
> > when he will ask me,
> > when he will ask you:
>
> I was lowly,
> did you help me to move up,
> to develop?
> I was hungry,
> what did you do?
> I was thirsty,
> where were you?
> I was in prison,
> sick, destitute, unemployed,

    bereaved, harassed, exploited,
    frustrated, beaten up, swindled,
    and you,
        where were you?
Let us be
where the action is,
let us be
where God's action
is.
Let us be.

Magendo mafia: smuggling, blackmarketing and profiteering in general.

44.

HE TURNED ON
HIS FOLLOWERS

Luke 14:25–33

He had said:
don't invite the rich,
the well-to-do;
don't invite your friends,
don't invite your family
but invite the poor,
    the crippled,
    the lame,
    the blind.
It is obvious
from the reports on Jesus' activity
that those poor,
    those crippled,
    those lame,
    those blind,
were the ones
who followed
him.
    The rich
    did not follow
    him,

the rich invited
him
to their tables,
yes,
but walking behind
him,
no.
The rich young man
wanted to follow him
while remaining rich,
but he left him
in the end.
The Pharisees
did not follow him,
they came to him
to ask questions,
to trap him,
but after those questions
they went home
to plot
and intrigue.
The learned professors
did not follow him,
even his academic friend Nicodemus
called him in the middle of the night
at his home
when he was in need of some
advice.
No,
the people who followed him,
who ran behind him,
who touched him,
who stepped on his heels
and did not leave him
any place
to sleep
were those poor,
those crippled,
those lame and
those blind.

They followed him
in droves,
in crowds
everywhere he went.
They put badges
on their tunics:
"Jesus loves
us"
      —they did not wear
      crosses,
      they did not know
      about that cross
      as yet—
they filled the streets,
the squares,
the corners,
the fields,
the lakeside
around him.
      When Jesus spoke about
      those rich
      who did not follow him
      they cheered
      and shouted:
      "Point,"
      and their equivalent of
      "Capitalists."
        When Jesus spoke about
        those Pharisees
        they enjoyed it
        very much.
        When he called them
        "hollow,"
        "hypocrites" and
        "whitewashed tombs,"
        they shouted:
        "Hear,
        hear!"
      They felt *firm,*
      they felt *called,*

they felt *safe,*
they felt *secure,*
they felt *saved,*
they felt *redeemed,*
they felt *honored,*
they felt *divine,*
    but then
    all at once
    in the Gospel of today
    Jesus turned on
    them
    abruptly.
They had been running
behind him,
they had been facing
the world
and its iniquity
together,
with him
so to speak
in front of them.
When he pointed his finger
at the evil
in front of them,
they would use their fingers too
to point in the same
direction.
    But now,
    suddenly,
    he turned around
    and faced
    them,
        not the rich,
        not the scribes,
        not the Pharisees,
    but them,
    and he said:
        "What about you?
        I know you like me
        to condemn the others;

> I know you like me
> to shout at them,
> but you,
> who call yourselves
> my followers,
> with your badges
> and your slogans,
> your new names
> and alleluias,
> what about you?
> Are you really
> willing to follow me,
> or would you
> in the final instance
> prefer your own life,
> your own sisters,
> your own brothers,
> your own wife,
> your own husband,
> your own father,
> your own mother?
> Are you really
> willing to carry
> my cross?
> You follow me
> but did you think
> about the towers
> we have to build?
> About the enemies
> we have to overcome?
> You are following me,
> you run behind me,
> you shout at the others
> who do not follow me;
> but are you honest
> with yourselves,
> are you really
> prepared
> to go my way
> all the way?"

He looked at them,
they looked at him
and a silence
suddenly
fell.

45.

THE TRIUMPH OF THE CROSS

John 3:13–17

There is a sudden interruption
in the flow of the
after-Pentecost Sundays
and the after-Pentecost Gospel readings.
Today we celebrate a feast,
a commemoration:
the triumph of the cross
and the suffering of Jesus Christ.
> And as this feast
> is about suffering
> it touches on one of the
> rawest nerves in our
> human existence.
> Suffering is something
> we all know about
> from within and
> from without.
> It is the greatest problem
> and the greatest scandal
> we carry with us.
Even the most unphilosophical person,
even the one who never asks any why,

will ask that
WHY
when confronted with suffering:
> Why did I fail,
> while all the others passed
> and I prayed so much?
>> Why did that car accident
>> happen to him
>> while so many other cars
>> drive on?
> Why did that infectious bug
> bite me
> and make me sick,
> a mother of so many?
>> Why can't I stop drinking
>> while others can easily
>> do without?
> Why do I starve?
> Why am I thirsty?
> Why do I find no work?
> Why did he betray me?
> Why did she go away?
>> All the disasters,
>> the natural ones
>> and the human-made ones,
>> the earthquakes
>> and the wars
>> and finally death itself
>> are accompanied
>> by that question
>> even Jesus Christ could not help
>> shouting from the cross:
>> "Why did you,
>> O God,
>> forsake me?"

And now
we are invited
to exalt
that suffering
of Christ

and, of course,
if we exalt his suffering
we should do the same
for our suffering
too.

      I think
      that we really should not
      glorify that suffering
      at all.
      There is no glory
      in pain as such.
      There is no glory
      in suffering
      at all.

Suffering does not even seem
to lead to anything.
It only seems to get worse,
even if it slips away
now and then.
If Jesus
would be only
a sympathetic companion
on this, our way of the cross,
he would not give us
very much hope
either.

      If Jesus
      had come only
      to participate
      in our lot
      and nothing more,
      then our hanging of crosses
      in our rooms all over the world,
      putting them on mountaintops
      and church steeples
      would be a very bitter
      mere underlining
      of the disaster
      we are participating
      in.

But we know
that that is not all.
We know that Jesus
went through his suffering
fighting it like
hell,
    healing left, right, and center,
    chasing out devils and evil spirits,
    raising people from death
    and making them see, smell, taste, touch, and hear,
    pointing out what went wrong
        politically,
        economically,
        socially,
        and religiously,
    and when finally
    the evil he tried to cope with
    caught up with him
    and arrested,
        tortured,
        and killed
        him,
    he shouted that last cry:
    "Father,
    why did you forsake
    me?"
        His Father answered
        not by words
        but by deeds,
        putting him
        again among us
        victoriously.
It is at this point
that we should understand
the meaning of our own suffering:
we should see our pain
as the result of our part
in the fight
to overcome it
once and for all.

Our pain will not be
in vain.
>If we see our suffering
>like that,
>if we endure it
>with that understanding,
>then we can use the
>*sign of his cross*
>to indicate that the fight
>will be
>won,
>in the risen life
>our way of the cross
>is leading us
>to.

46.

ON DIRTYING YOUR HANDS

Luke 16:1–13

The notice had come
that morning.
The manager just
had heard
that he was going
to be investigated.
He had a moment
of panic,
it would mean his
dismissal.
His double-dealing
would be discovered.
He had no doubt
about that.
A court case
was unavoidable.
But then he sat down
behind his desk.
He had no time
to lose.
Friends would be more necessary
than ever before.

He needed protection.
He needed help.
He needed support.
He called the auditors
of his master.
He told them
to sit down.
He explained to them
his predicament.
He said:
"Now the books
can still be changed.
Tomorrow might be
too late.
What percentage
do you give me
if I change
them?"

Amounts were
mentioned.
Some haggling
took place.
Affairs were
settled,
erasers and rubbers
used
and finally the books
were
closed.
His boss could
come.
Everything had been dealt with
in time.

And Jesus said,
after having told
this story,
known all over Jerusalem
because it had really
happened,

that he admired
the presence of mind
of that accountant.
He did not panic.
He did not faint.
He did not lose
a minute.
He kept wide
awake.
He did not lament,
but took action
immediately.
>He asked them:
>"Why don't you act
>like that caretaker
>when it comes to
>the kingdom affairs
>I entrusted to you?"
He did not mean to say
that we should act
unfairly
in view of the kingdom.
He asked us
to act as quickly
and as efficiently
as that caretaker
in the situations
we meet.
>He foresaw
>an obvious objection
>why we might decide
>not to act
>in this world.
Is this world
not a place
of darkness?
Are all its structures
not corrupt?
Is not everything
tainted with evil?

Would it not be better
if we retired totally
out of all public life
    socially,
    politically,
    and economically?
Should we not keep ourselves
pure
and without stain?
    His answer was:
    "No,
    you should not abstain,
    use money,
    use all you have,
    tainted as it is,
    to win you friends,
    and thus make sure
    that when it fails you,
    they will welcome you
    into the tents
    of eternity."
    We cannot escape
    from the evil
    in this world.
    We cannot keep
    our hands clean,
    but we are not allowed
    to keep them in our pockets
    either.
    We have to take the risks
    he took
    in order
    to change us
    all.

47.

ON NOT DIRTYING
YOUR HANDS

Luke 16:19–31

Jesus said:
"There was a rich man."
We often add
that he was mean.
Jesus did not say that
and besides he did not seem mean
at all.
He spent his money
lavishly.
But he spent it
on himself:
> dressed in purple
> according to the latest
> fashion,
> underwear in the finest
> linen,
> beautiful meals,
> ten-course dinners,
> candlelight all over,
> soft music in the background,

vintage wines,
ice-cooled imported
beers.
He was not mean,
but he was not hospitable
either,
he seemed to have
wined and dined
alone.
Jesus did not say
that he was bad.
We often add
that he was bad.
In fact that rich man
was not bad
at all.
He allowed
that poor man Lazarus
to lie at his door
day and night
notwithstanding the sores.
Who of us
would allow that
on our own premises?
Wouldn't you call
the police?
Jesus does not say
that Lazarus did not get
the scraps that fell
from his table.
We say so,
but not he.
In some translations
it is added
that no one gave him
those scraps,
but maybe this meant
that he had to fetch them
himself,

creeping under the table
together with the dogs
when the servants
came to clean up
after the meals.
        Jesus describes
        the poor man Lazarus
        as totally destitute,
        totally helpless.
        He lay,
        since he could not sit
        or stand.
        He was full of sores
        and the dogs
            —while waiting for
            the scraps—
        came to lick his wounds,
        which means
        that he even had not the power
        to keep those dogs
        away from himself.
Though not bad,
and in the eyes of himself
and the others
very tolerant
and charitable,
the rich man
made one mistake.
        He did not want
        to dirty his hands.
        He did not take any
        action
        to improve
        the poor man's lot.
        He allowed him on his
        premises,
        he allowed him to search
        for scraps
        in his dustbins,

but he overlooked the point
the dishonest caretaker
did not overlook
last Sunday.
He did not make himself
friends.
He did not really care
for the life-process
that was dying off
in the running sores
of Lazarus.
It was that lack
of care
that created a distance
that grew
from day to day,
though they lived
in the same world
and in the same compound,
between him and
Lazarus.
And when they both
finally died
that distance was still
the gulf that separated
those two.
The rich man
had not shared
his life
with anyone.
He had not been
mean,
he had not been
bad,
he had been
alone
though the other
was
there.

He had not wanted
to dirty his hands
and now even the tip
of a finger
he asked for
was refused.
The distance
had become
too great.

48.

VISION COMES SLOWLY

Luke 17:5–10

The prophet Habakkuk
lived very,
very long ago.
It was very,
very long ago
that he got his vision
and that he shouted
to God:
> "Why do I see
> what I see?
> Why do I see
> injustice;
> why do you,
> God,
> tolerate
> tyranny
> and outrage
> and violence
> and contention
> and discord?
> Why?"

Those shouts,
those very cries
come,
now and then
and rather often,
from our very own lips
too.
        Why is it
        that everything
        seems to turn sour
        all the time?
Why is it
that injustice
and stupidity
seem to prevail
everywhere?
        The prophet asked
        for an answer;
        he asked
        for an explanation;
        he asked
        for understanding;
        he asked
        for a belief;
        he asked
        for vision;
        he asked
        to be saved
        in his hope
        and in his faith.
            The answer
            from God
            came
            and the answer was:
            "Don't be afraid,
            the vision
            will come
            in time.

It might be slow
but come
it will."
Very,
very many years later
Jesus' disciples
came to him
with the same question,
surrounded as they were
by the disastrous world
in which they lived,
aware of the fights
they themselves
had already had
about the first place
and issues like that.
   They too said:
   "A vision,
   give us vision;
   faith,
   we need faith;
   hope,
   give us hope;
   light,
   let us see;
   increase
   our faith."
      How often
      do we not ask ourselves
      for that faith,
      for that hope,
      for that vision.
      We do ask,
      and yet . . .
      aren't we blocking
      that vision and
      that faith
      at the same time?

Aren't we the reason
that
vision
comes so slowly,
so very,
very slowly?
Because we know
perfectly well
that in that vision
and in that faith
   we would see
   how far
   we ourselves
   are the cause and the reason
   of the disasters
   and the injustices,
   of the violence
   and the oppression
   around us
   in this world.
We ask for faith,
but we refuse to believe;
we ask for light
but we prefer the dark;
   —useless
   servants.
But then he speaks,
and he says:
"Even if your faith
would be like a mustard seed,
so small,
you would be able
to move the world,
the mountains
and the trees
with roots and all
and yourselves
too."

It is that faith
and that movement,
that change
and that turn,
we need.
It is the risk
we have to
take.

49.

NOT THE LAW BUT HIS LOVE

Luke 17:11–19

Ten lepers
came out of the village.
A conspiracy of the sick
looking for health.
     They remained
     standing at a distance.
     They did as foreseen
     by the law.
     They hailed him,
     and shouted
     through their hands
     as foreseen
     by the law:
     "Jesus,
     Master,
      take pity
     on us."
He stopped
and looked at them
keeping his distance
as foreseen
by the law.

274

He did not touch
them,
he did not approach
them.
He too,
that day,
stuck to the law,
even when he ordered
them:
"Go,
and show yourselves
to the priests"
as was stipulated
for anyone
who claimed
to be healed
from his skin disease.
     They did
     what he said,
     though they were not
     healed
     as yet.
     They walked away
     full of hope,
     full of faith.
       Suddenly their skins
       started to work,
       the shape of their fingers and toes,
       of their noses and lips,
       of their ears and their eyelids
       started to
       readjust.
       The sick colors
       disappeared,
       their bodies started
       to glow and to shine
       in a newly acquired
       tautness.
       They were healed.

They started
to run
faster and faster
in the direction
of the temple
to get through
all the rites and observances
as soon as possible
to join their families,
    their occupations,
    their businesses,
    and their lives.
They must have arrived
out of breath
when presenting
themselves
to the priestly
temple health board.
    But during
    that race
    they had lost
    one among them.
    One had turned
    around
    running in the
    opposite direction,
    running toward Jesus,
    forgetting about
    all those observances
    and regulations.
He ran back
to Jesus
praising God
at the top
of his voice,
throwing himself
at his feet
and thanking him
for his
salvation.

And it was to him,
and to him alone,
the disobedient one,
the one who had not done
what he had been told to do,
the one who broke through
the obligation of the law,
that Jesus said:
"Stand up
and go,
your faith
has saved you."
The others
were healed,
this one
was saved.
The others
found their families,
    their occupations,
    their businesses,
    and their lives;
this one found
his Redeemer.
Immediately after this episode
there is verse 20
in the seventeenth chapter of Luke.
That verse can be translated in two ways.
It can read:
*"the coming of the kingdom
cannot be observed";*
it can read:
*"the kindgom of God
does not consist in
observance."*
It is
Jesus' love
for human life
that will reign
and nothing
else.

50.

HOW PRAYERS ARE HEARD

Luke 18:1–8

The story in the first reading
from Exodus today
is a very old story
and it is one that repeats itself
all the time:
  the people of God
  were attacked by evil forces.
Moses said:
"I will pray to God,
with my staff in my hand
on that hilltop over there,
to let us win."
  That is what he did,
  his hands high up,
  his staff in his right hand,
  a living sign
  of someone imploring God.
But the fight lasted
and lasted,
the sun shone,
Moses was old,

278

his staff became heavier and heavier,
his legs pained
and his hands came down,
his right hand first,
and immediately
his people started to lose
and they shouted to him:
"Keep those hands up,
pray";
and when his hands went up again
they gained the upper hand,
but he could not keep the staff up
anymore
and his hands went down again,
his right hand first,
and again they started to lose
until Aaron and Hur
came to help him.

> They put him on a stone,
> Aaron took his right hand
> and kept it up,
> Hur took his left hand
> and kept it up,
> and Moses remained praying
> until sunset,
> until the battle was over
> and won.

A story obviously
about the power of prayer,
and the story Jesus tells us
in the Gospel
seems to teach the same
lesson.
Luke even remarks before
telling it
that it is about the need
to pray
continually and never
lose heart.

That is what that widow
definitely did not do
when she went again and again
to that judge
to get justice done.
That judge in the story of Jesus
was so powerful
and so rich
and so well protected
that he did not fear any human
being.
He could buy,
he could blackmail them all.
He had sufficient money
and sufficient incriminating information
to silence anybody.
He was,
said Jesus,
not even afraid of
God.
But when that widow
came asking him,
praying him again and again,
again and again
and again
to do justice to her,
he gave up.
He said:
"I might not be afraid of God
or man,
but that widow
will be my end,
she will pester me to death,
let me do her justice."
Two stories
about the power of prayer.
Two stories about prayers heard
plus
Jesus' assurance
that our prayers,

especially the ones
for justice
in our terribly unjust world,
will be heard.
        But those stories
        are not only about praying.
        They are not only about the fact
        that our prayers will be heard,
        they are also about
        HOW
        our prayers will be heard.
While Moses prayed
he had to struggle
to keep his hands up.
God interfered
by helping him to do that.
While Moses prayed
the others were fighting
in order that justice might be done.
        God saw to it
        that justice was done
        but God did not interfere
        directly,
        he equipped his people,
        he equipped Moses,
        he equipped the widow
        with all that was necessary
        to have their prayers
        heard.
These stories are
about the necessity to pray,
right,
they are about the need
to persevere in prayer,
right,
but they are also about the fact
that those prayers
are going to be heard
by us,
who are,

according to the second reading of today,
the one from that letter of Saint Paul
to Timothy:
>   *"fully equipped*
>   *and ready for any good work";*
we need not only to pray,
we need to work.

>   Let me give you an example
>   of what I want to say.
>   You all have heard
>   about that terrible earthquake
>   ten days ago
>   in El Asnan,
>   Algeria.
>   In a matter of a few seconds
>   up to twenty thousand people
>   were killed.

I think that every one of us
must have asked himself or herself
that same question:
"How can God
allow such a thing?"

>   A very difficult question indeed,
>   especially when you hear
>   that the quake
>   came on a Friday,
>   while very many were
>   at their midmorning prayers
>   in the mosque.

Why?
There had been another earthquake
in the very same town
in 1954.
Not so many were killed
at that time,
the town was then not
so large,
only about
fifteen hundred.

One knew that the town
was built on a geological fault,
that new earthquakes might occur.
That is why,
when rebuilding the town,
laws were passed
to construct earthquake-resistant buildings,
but the people who built,
the contractors and the architects,
the landlords and the investors,
did not adhere to those laws.
One prayed for protection,
one prayed for blessings,
and one prayed in that town
definitely, regularly,
against disasters and earthquakes
but one did not make
the effort,
or one did not make
sufficient effort,
to have one's prayers
heard.
Let us pray,
let us continue to pray
that justice may be done,
but let us also
do justice;
let us be on
OUR MISSION
as Paul wrote:
"I put this duty to you
in the name of his appearing
and his kingdom:
proclaim the message,
and welcome or unwelcome
insist on it,
refute falsehood,
correct error,
call to obedience."

Pray,
but
do not only expect God's intervention,
God will intervene
but through you,
through us,
equipped with his word,
    his power, and
    his Spirit.
    Amen.

51.

PRAYING FOR MERCY

Luke 18:9–14

There are those two men in the temple,
one the Pharisee,
with his nose in the air,
his chest blown up,
his eyes fixed on heaven,
pointing at himself
while praying to himself:
    "God,
    here I am,
    aren't you happy?
    Your churchman,
    your faithful contributor
    to all church causes,
    Lord,
    look at me
    your own running religious
    success story
    in this town."
And the other,
the tax collector,
his nose pointing to the earth,
his eyes down,

285

his chest sunk,
beating his breast
praying to God:
        "Please, Lord, please,
        look down on me,
        a sinful wretch,
        I don't dare to lift
        my eyes up to you,
        but look down on me,
        sorry,
        have mercy on
        me."
It is a story
we all know,
the churchgoers
because they come to church,
and the nonchurchgoers
because they very often use this story
to justify their not going to church.
They don't want to sit down,
they say,
with all those hypocrites in church
and they forget
that that tax collector
was in church
too.
        It is a story
        about hypocrisy;
        it is a story about
        how to pray and about
        how not to pray.
        It is a story that can be read
        in other ways
        as well.
That Pharisee
lived in the same town
as the tax collector,
that Pharisee
lived in the same time
as the tax collector.

They both stood
in the same temple,
at the same hour,
he in front,
the other one in the back.
        They were both convinced
        that their town,
        that their days
        and their world
        were evil:
            greedy,
            unjust,
            and adulterous.
        But in that sinful world
        they each prayed
        in a different way.
The Pharisee
asked God
to recognize his virtue
and his righteousness,
though the world around him
was so sinful.
        The tax collector
        asked God
        to have a good look at him,
        a sinner,
        and to have mercy on him,
        because he
        and the world around him
        were so bad.
Jesus evaluated the prayers
of both
and he said
that the prayer of the tax collector
was good
and the prayer of the Pharisee
bad.
        Why?
        There are, I think,
        very many reasons for that.

Let us have a look
at one of those reasons
only.
Just imagine that all Christians,
that all religious people
in this country
and in this world
would pray like the Pharisee:
"Here I am,
I am good
and I detest the world
for its sinfulness."
If we all would pray like that,
how would this world
ever,
ever change?
The Pharisee himself
was not going to change
because he declared himself good already,
and the world would not change
because of him
as he only detested it.
And then
just imagine that all Christians,
that all religious people
in this country
and in this world
would pray like the tax collector:
"Please, Lord, please,
have mercy on me
and on the world."
Do you think
that in that case
this world would remain
the same?
Jesus said:
"That Pharisee
went home
unchanged,
a dead loss,

useless for himself,
useless to the world,
a closed door,
locked,
double-locked,
and bolted,
no way,
a dead end."
     And Jesus said:
     "That tax collector
     went home
     changed,
     justified,
     right with God,
     an open door,
     a new future,
     hope,
     change."
We need that prayer
of the tax collector
more and more
for ourselves,
for each other,
for this world,
we need
God's mercy
on this campus,
in this country
maybe even more
than ever before,
     because of the greed,
     because of the injustices,
     because of the adulterated
     human relationships.
Yet,
when we pray
for that so-much-needed mercy
we should understand
how that prayer
will be heard.

We should not expect
that God in his mercy
will come down
to purify,
to rectify
or to adjust the lot.
    When we pray in the "Our Father"
    for our daily bread,
    we don't expect that
    God,
    to hear that prayer,
    will open a big bakery in heaven,
    raining down
    loaves and rolls,
    cakes and biscuits,
    parcels of *ugali* and *unga**
        —though he did even that
        for some time when they
        were in the desert—
    with words written on them,
    not:
    "made in Kenya,"
    but:
    "manufactured and packed
    in heaven,
    untouched by human hands,
    by God and his angels."
        When we pray for bread
        we expect God to give us rain
        and fertility
        and a good harvest,
        but we know that our prayer
        can only be heard
        if we ourselves
        are willing to work,
        to plow and to harvest,
        to grind and to bake,
        and to distribute the food produced
        with equity and justice.

When we pray for God's mercy
it is the same.
When we pray for mercy
God will hear us
by sending
his Spirit
and his power
by sending
God's mercy
in us,
    so that *we* can overcome
    all that unkindness
    and greed,
    all those injustices
    and adultery.
When we pray for God's mercy
God will hear our prayers,
he will send his gracefulness
down on us
so that we can be merciful
and careful
and respectful
to each other
    in the traffic,
    when queuing up for essentials,
    when distributing what we have
    mercifully.

Ugali: a thick porridge; *Unga:* flour.

52.

PRAYING FOR THE DEAD

Matthew 25:31–46

You must have been
at very many funerals.
You must have heard
very many speeches and talks
at those funerals.
You must have noticed
something very peculiar
about all those words
at those occasions.
      I did,
      but you must have
      too.
      There was that funeral
      of that man
      who only thought of his business
      day and night,
      that man who thought so much
      about making money
      that he almost looked
      like a banknote,
      but at his funeral
      nobody said a word
      about that;

he was,
they said,
such a loving husband
and so caring for his
children
and like an open hand
to all those
in need.
And one simply
starts to wonder!
Suddenly
there is no doubt
about goodness;
there is no hestitation
about mercy,
there is no doubt
about charity:
he should go straight
to heaven,
      and yet
      when the tears are dried up,
      when the coffin is covered with sand,
      when the flowers start to wither
      in the sun,
      when the last visitor
      has left
      and everyone returned
      to the world
      in which
      that beloved dead person
      had lived
      for so long
      with them,
      they will also
      find in that world
      the harm he did
      whether the eulogist
      at the funeral
      mentioned it
      or not.

And we really face a problem
when we see the life of that man
in the light of the Gospel
of today.
>Was he good
>or was he bad?
>Was he a sheep
>or was he a goat?
>Is he a saint
>or is he a sinner?
>Does he belong
>to the right,
>or does he belong
>to the left?
He did feed
some hungry
during his life,
but he refused to feed
so many others.
He did quench the thirst
of some,
but he left so many
thirsty.
He did visit some prisoners
but he refused to visit others.
He did dress some naked,
he did not dress
some others.
He did meet Christ
in others
several times,
he refused to meet him
in others
so very many times!
>What will Christ do
>sitting there as a judge
>on his high throne
>before the whole assembly
>of humankind
>in such a case

when confronted
with that mixture
of good and bad,
of splendor and squalor,
half sheep, half goat,
what will he do?
But will not all of us
be in that very same situation?
Are not all of us that mixture?
Do we not all know
that we are surrounded
by those hungry,
by those thirsty,
by those naked,
by those imprisoned
while we help
only some of them
now and then?
And that is why
all of us,
once we stand in front of that throne,
will be but too willing
to forgive those who did
real harm to us
in this world.
Because we are all guilty,
because we are all at fault,
because we all betrayed each other,
because we all need forgiveness
and without that forgiveness
all of us should be standing
on the left,
with only Mary his mother
and maybe Joseph
standing on the right.
Today we commemorate all souls.
We pray for those
of whom we think
that they might not yet be
in the full company of God

as their sins
here on earth
are still with us
and frustrate even now
our lives:
>the teeth kicked out by them
>are still kicked out,
>the scars of the wounds
>made by them
>did not yet heal,
>the psychological harm they did
>still mars
>our minds.
>Today we pray
>for them,
>but our prayer makes sense
>only inasfar as we are willing
>to forgive them
>and inasfar as we ask God
>to do the same.
>>All Souls is a day
>>of mercy,
>>of universal mercy,
>>a day of forgiveness,
>>but it should also be
>>the day
>>to review
>>our own lives
>>in such a way
>>that goodness and sanctity
>>may prevail more
>>and more.

53.

ON LIFE AFTER DEATH

Luke 20:27–38

They came to Jesus
sniggering.
They were sure
that they were going
to catch him in his words.
> The question was about
> life after death,
> the question was about
> the resurrection.
> They had decided
> among themselves
> that there was no life
> after death,
> because they said:
> "The consequences of life
> after death are
> ridiculous,
> totally absurd.
> Where would you put
> all those people,
> how would you feed them,

how would you be able to cater
to all those human relations
messed up so thoroughly
here on earth?"
And they had found
the example
of that poor lady
who for seven times
in succession
embraced a dying husband
in her bed
to see him part
before any fruit
had set.

They did not start
with their real issue;
they started with that widow
and those seven husbands
one after another.
It was only
at the end
that they said:
"Now what is going to happen
after her death
and resurrection
and after the resurrection
of those seven?
How is she going
to relate to them,
how is she going
to manage,
how is she going
to divide her time?"

And they laughed
already
knowing
that the answer
would not
come.

It did not
come.
He even overlooked
their question.
He asked them
another
one.
He asked them
about four people
who went before
them:

> Abraham,
> Isaac,
> Jacob, and
> Moses,

and he asked them:
"Do you really think
that those men of God
died,
do you really think
that God made them disappear
into clouds of nothingness,
into the dark of oblivion?
Do you really think
that God,
who loved them
so much,
who influenced their lives
so much,
would have forgotten those
you
even
remember?
Do you really think
that God is a God
of dead people,
of some life-moments only,
of some green wood
that dried up

to be thrown away
and burned
in a fire,
to turn into
dust and ashes?
Do you really think
that God will disavow them,
overlook them,
or forget them?
You must be joking!"

      "Is that what you think?
      Wouldn't that be absurd?
      Wouldn't that be unbelievable?
      Can you think of yourself
      as being overlooked in the end,
      after your struggles,
      after your frustrations,
      after your moments of happiness,
      after your moments of greatness?
      You must be joking!"

But,
brothers and sisters,
listen carefully
to the names he mentions:
      Abraham,
      Isaac,
      Jacob, and
      Moses.
Listen carefully
to what he says:
      "Those who are judged
      worthy!"
Let us not deceive ourselves
about Jesus,
let us not deceive ourselves
about ourselves:
the life
that awaits us
hereafter
is our own life:

the consequence
of what we *did*
here on earth.
>   We should be here
>   on earth
>   living in the line
>   of Abraham,
>   of Jacob,
>   of Isaac,
>   of Moses, and
>   of Jesus Christ,
>   and we will
>   live
>   forever and ever.

54.

YOUR ENDURANCE WILL WIN YOU YOUR LIVES

Luke 21:5–19

The last days of a year
are days of evaluations,
of surveys,
and of reports on activities,
on successes and failures.
   Jesus gives such
   a report on the last days
   and it seems that all went
   wrong.
   He mentions: wars,
    revolutions,
    fights of nations against nations,
    fights of kingdoms against kingdoms,
    earthquakes,
    plague,
    famine,
    fearful sights,
    signs from heaven,
    arrests,
    persecutions,

interrogations,
imprisonments,
and for some even
executions.
And when his disciples
to offset all that grimness
point to the temple
with its whites and golds
glittering in the sun,
he simply says:
"Don't be mistaken,
all that will be destroyed also,
not a single stone
will remain
on another."
There seems to be a mood
of almost total depression.
All the seed sown
seems to be overgrown again
by weeds.
All the links
binding together human relations
seem to be broken.
All efforts were in vain.
Injustice reigns.
The *mafia* rules.
Magendo * was not overcome.
The murderers are still with us.
The end is near.
What to do?
Once the Jews
had been in a situation
like that before.
It was during their
Babylonian exile.
All hope was finished,
any possible future squashed,
men and women were separated,
the birth of children hardly tolerated,

no songs were heard,
who sings in prison?
Life went on
in a kind of semidark.
All that went on before
seemed to have been in vain,
Moses and the exodus from Egypt
included.
They were hopeless,
desperate, depressed.
It was not worthwhile to get
out of your bed in the morning.
One activity, however, went on.
A very strange one.
In the dark corners
of their existence
scribes were going round
to record the stories
from the past,
pieces of oral tradition,
scraps of written documents.
They collected them all
and wrote during those exile years
the final redaction
of the first books
of the Bible.
It was in that chaos,
it was during that depression
that Genesis was written
as a remedy against
despair,
the last straw of an old hope,
the first straw of a new beginning.
Those Jews
in the dark,
oppressed,
in chaos,
wrote:

In the beginning
there was chaos,
a formless void,
darkness over the deep,
until God spoke
and the dark was separated
from the light
and the earth
from the water.
New life crawled
through the water
and over the earth,
    trees started flowering,
    birds started whistling,
    flowers started blooming
    and Adam looked for Eve
    and Eve found Adam.
And God looking at his work
after the first day,
after the second day,
after the third day,
after the fourth day,
after the fifth day,
and after the sixth day,
saw that it was all made
well
and he took a rest
the seventh day.
In that story
the Jews expressed
their fundamental belief
and their faith
in their hope.
    Depression
    seems to be the mood
    of our days.
    Weeds that were thrown out
    at the right

grow up again
at the left.
Dangers once local
are becoming
global.
The weapons pile
is getting higher
and higher.
Human relationships seem
to disintegrate
more and more,
the old homesteads
are gone.
Persons dissolve
in loyalty crises.
Money does not buy
anything
anymore.
But now
we are here
telling each other
the story of Jesus
remembering his deeds,
his suffering,
yes,
but his resurrection
too.
       And he tells us
       to endure
       and he assures us
       that life will be ours.
Yesterday
a boy of about fourteen
told me:
"God will get tired
with this world,
he will destroy it,
I am sure.

People will turn
into ants
and the sun will fall
down."
I am not so sure,
we should not be too sure
of that.
As that African bishop said
at a synod in Rome:
"Every newly born child
is seen by us
as a sign of God's lasting
confidence
in this world!"
We will win,
we will overcome.
Our endurance,
our work,
our prayers,
our efforts,
our attempts
will win us
our lives.

Magendo: smuggling, blackmarketing, and profiteering in general.

55.

THE WAY JESUS RULES

Luke 23:35–43

When celebrating
the Kingship
of Jesus Christ
the Gospel reading
brings us today
to the most painful
and apparently
the most powerless moment
in his life.
> He is hanging
> on the cross,
> bleeding to death.
> People are staring at him,
> interested in seeing him
> die.
> Priests shout at him
> in their last efforts
> to get a confession
> from him,
>> those priests
>> were not necessarily
>> cruel,

they had according to Jewish law
to accompany anyone condemned
to death,
so that in case the executed person
would confess his guilt
they would be there
to assure him
of God's mercy.
But the presence of those priests
must have manifested to Jesus
up to the last moment
how he had been misunderstood.
The soldiers
had put a crown of thorns
on his head,
and to explain that crown
they had put that notice
above his head:
"King of the Jews,"
not so much to pester him
but to humiliate the Jews.
The sky was
overcast,
birds and animals
started hiding.
He had shouted for
God.
He had asked for
water.
He had seen
how even his clothing
had been carried
away already.
All glory
was gone,
he hung there
naked.
All dreams
had ended.

All hopes
were squashed.
Faith in him
had disappeared.
His disciples
were on the run.
Only his mother
and some women
were standing
at a distance.
John would return
in the last minute
only.
The sun turned
its face
away from
this scene;
it got very,
very dark.
He was not alone
in his agony.
Two criminals
were hanging
next to him.
One of the two
turned against him.
The second one
did not.
He turned to Jesus
and said:
"We are hanging here
because we were bad.
We are hanging here
because we spoiled the world.
But you are hanging here
because you were good.
You are hanging here
because you wanted to
correct the world."

He did not say that
to mock him,
like the others.
He said it
because he believed
in him.
And Jesus turned,
with his very last power,
his head:
finally he had found
a companion,
finally he had found
some hope,
    the new beginning,
    the only stepping-stone
    into his kingdom.
He said:
"I promise you,
today
you will be with me
in paradise."
    At the moment
    that he spoke those words,
    his kingdom
    had in a way
    contracted to that
    one man
    next to him only,
    the smallest possible base
    for the things to come,
    one changed human heart,
    the heart of a former
    crook.
    The start of the
    new dawn.
In today's second reading
Paul
calls Jesus
the image of the unseen God,

the seen God among us,
the firstborn of all creation,
in him all things had been made
in heaven and on earth,
visible and invisible,
Thrones,
Dominations,
Sovereignties,
Powers,
he existed before
anything else,
he keeps it all
together,
he is the head of
creation,
he is the head of
the body,
the head of
the church,
he is the beginning,
the end,
and all perfection.
      He is,
      he was,
      and he will be
      king.
            There,
            on the cross,
            all this was fulfilled
            at the moment
            that he accepted that man
            next to him
            who believed
            in his kingdom.
                  That was the way
                  his kingdom got established
                  here on earth;
                  that is how he got a grip
                  over this world.

If each one of us
would tell him
what that thief asked him:
"Remember me,
I want to be with you,"
then this world would change,
we would find each other
in his body
and if we would be
consequent
his reign would start
among all of us.
    It is only beginning
    from our hearts
    that paradise can start;
    it is only from our hearts
    that things can really
    change.
It is the option
of that thief
that builds
the bridge between
here and there,
the bridge between
now and then.
    And with that conclusion
    we are ready
    to be on the lookout
    for him
    again.
    We can start a new year
    hoping that he will
    come
    more and more.
    AMEN.

INDEX OF SCRIPTURAL TEXTS